Practical Guide to SAP® GTS Edition for SAP HANA®

Part I: SPL Screen and Compliance Management

2nd edition

Kevin Riddell
Rajen Iyer
Mouli Venkataraman

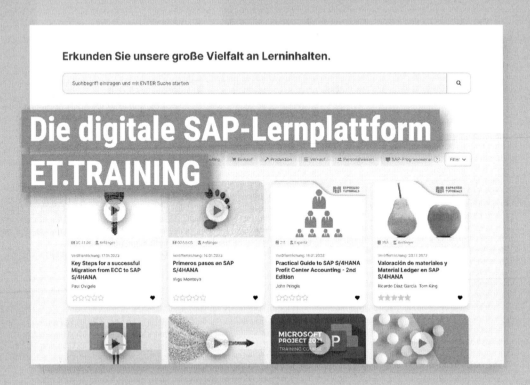

Die digitale SAP-Lernplattform ET.TRAINING

Qualifizieren Sie Ihre Mitarbeiter
ohne Reisekosten und externe Referenten

- ▸ 800+ E-Books und Videos in den Sprachen DE, EN, FR, PT, JP, ES

- ▸ Über 40 Lernpfade erleichtern die Einarbeitung in neue SAP-Themen

- ▸ Laufende Aktualisierung mit neuen Inhalten

- ▸ Zugang via Webbrowser oder App (iOS/Android)

- ▸ Staffelpreise ab 5 Lizenzen

Die Lernplattform:
https://et.training

7-Tage-Testzugang kostenfrei und unverbindlich:
https://et.training/testzugang

Individuelles Angebot für Firmen:
https://www.espresso-tutorials.de/firmenkunden/

Vielen Dank an unsere Sponsoren beim GTS Forum 2023!

Deloitte.

Das internationale SAP Global Trade Services (SAP GTS) Team von Deloitte unterstützt Unternehmen bei der Entwicklung und Implementierung von Lösungen für komplexe Handelsanforderungen. In den letzten 15 Jahren hat Deloitte ein marktführendes Serviceangebot für die weltweite Implementierung von SAP GTS entwickelt. Der Erfolg unseres Angebots zeichnet sich in der besonderen und einzigartigen Zusammensetzung unseres Teams aus. Spezialisten für globale Handelsvorschriften, Zoll- und Außenhandelsprozesse sowie fachliche und technische SAP GTS-Berater arbeiten Hand in Hand und betreuen unsere Kunden so mit einem multidisziplinären Ansatz.

Unser globales Team bietet Expertise in allen GTS-Funktionen und verfügt über umfangreiche Erfahrung in Neuimplementierungen, Systemkonvertierungen sowie Application Management Support (AMS). Auch in der Umstellung von GTS 11.0 auf GTS Edition for SAP HANA ist das Deloitte SAP GTS Team ihr richtiger Partner.

Neben dem umfassenden SAP GTS-Beratungsangebot hat Deloitte auch eigene IT-Ansätze entwickelt, die sich mit SAP GTS integrieren lassen, um Unternehmen bei multilateralen Handelsaktivitäten bestmöglich zu unterstützen. Unsere innovative IT-Lösung „Trade Classifier" automatisiert den komplexen Prozess der zolltariflichen Einreihung und optimiert so den Zollabwicklungsprozess. Durch den Einsatz des „Trade Classifier" können Unternehmen ihre Zollabwicklung optimieren, die Einhaltung der Zollvorschriften sicherstellen und mögliche Risiken bei der Import- und Exportverzollung reduzieren.

Mit mehr als 140 SAP GTS Implementierungen in über 70 Ländern weltweit sind Sie bei Deloitte in guten Händen.

Kevin Riddell, Rajen Iyer, Mouli Venkataraman
Practical Guide to SAP® GTS Edition for SAP HANA — Part I: SPL Screen and Compliance Management, 2nd edition

ISBN:	978-3-96012-225-8
Editor:	Montero Language Services
Cover Design:	Philip Esch
Cover Photo:	istockphoto.com | Tryaging No. 600688830
Interior Book Design:	Johann-Christian Hanke

All rights reserved.

2nd edition 2023, Gleichen

© 2023 by Espresso Tutorials GmbH

URL: *www.espresso-tutorials.com*

Feedback
We greatly appreciate any feedback you may have concerning this book. Please send your feedback via email to: *info@espresso-tutorials.com*.

Table of Contents

Preface

Thank you for purchasing Book 1 of the Practical Guide to SAP GTS Edition for SAP HANA. Our practical guide is the first of its kind for GTS. Similar guides have been written for other SAP modules, but we feel this addresses a very real business need for GTS users. If you are a current user, you already know that GTS is a powerful tool. This book will help you use this tool more efficiently, and maybe even learn about new aspects of the system you are unfamiliar with.

GTS is a compliance tool. For this reason, our practical guide offers not only software assistance, but also compliance assistance. We trust that the material will assist you as you develop and/or review your company's compliance programs. We also offer suggestions on how to audit the effectiveness of your GTS installation—ensuring you can withstand any external audit should it ever occur.

Book 1 focuses on compliance management, with an in-depth review of sanctioned party list (SPL) screening in the new SAP GTS edition for HANA version. Book 2 covers customs management and preference processing. It is our hope that the multi-book format will allow you to choose the topics that interests you the most.

In addition to its core content, this book offers details of what is in store for the new SAP GTS Edition for SAP HANA. It includes several new topics and provides a review of the new Fiori-based Apps and UX (user experience) developments.

Thank you again and we sincerely hope this book helps make your life easier, and more compliant!

> **❗ Help!**
>
> The software implementation is complete, the go-live date has come and gone, and all of the users are trained. The team has disbanded, and everyone has returned to their regular duties. The celebration party is already a distant memory. You are a user responsible for SPL releases and reviews. So far, this experience has consisted of multiple false positives that you have released.

> You came into work this morning and found a "match" resulting in a blocked document. You review the block. For the first time since you began using the software, you think you may be looking at a real positive match! The customer on the order may actually be the entity on the SPL—now what?
>
> Unfortunately, too many users are put in this position and are never properly trained on what to do with the software now that they have it. Sure, they were trained on how to release the document. They also were shown how to place the customer on the negative list if it is a genuine match. However, they were never trained on the nuances of reviewing the SPL and how to deal with a "close match," or possible valid match.

Well, if this is you, this guide is here to help. Not just for SPL (Sanctioned Party Lists), but also for other key functions in SAP GTS Edition for SAP HANA. This book is the first of a two-part set. Part 1 focuses on compliance management and is divided into two parts—SPL and import/export compliance management. Part 2 focuses on customs management and preference processing.

There are several books on installing and configuring SAP GTS, but until now, none of those have focused on using GTS in a compliant manner. Installation and configuration are essential parts of a GTS implementation, but they are not the whole story. They also should not be the first tasks to take place in an implementation. They must be preceded by an understanding of the problems for which GTS provides a solution. You will only be able to maximize the value of an SAP GTS implementation by first conducting a thorough review of your business needs and a proper understanding of what GTS can do.

This book is meant to be a hybrid: while it is, of course, an SAP GTS manual, it is also serves as a compliance guide. SAP GTS is a software tool. The greater goal is not merely a software installation but the implementation of a complete trade compliance solution. This cannot be done solely in the area of a software implementation; it must accompany and be guided by compliance expertise. This book will help you both with a successful GTS implementation and with compliance.

This book will cover the following topics specific to SPL and compliance management:

▶ Understanding the regulatory requirements related to international trade compliance. These notes are focused primarily on the US but also touch on the requirements for other countries.

▶ Understanding how GTS can provide a solution to regulatory requirements.

▶ Reviews and walk-through of configuration, especially in situations where configuration choices could affect compliance levels.

▶ Tips on how to best leverage SAP GTS, including an overview of the key functions and the most commonly encountered user choices/ actions. This is not meant to be an exhaustive review of all functions, just those that the majority of users can expect to encounter.

▶ Compliance tips, including specific software tips and general compliance tips.

▶ Suggested business process flows to assist the reader in creating similar processes at their own company.

We will not cover all of the SAP GTS functionality available. Rather than give high-level coverage of all areas, we will instead offer in-depth assistance with the specific functions that the majority of users face. In each installation, the user is free to activate the functions they wish to use and leave others unused. Based on the majority of installations, the following four general functions are covered:

▶ Sanctioned party list screening (Book 1)

▶ Compliance management (Book 1)

▶ Preference processing (Book 2)

▶ Customs management (Book 2)

Each book also includes a section on SAP GTS Edition for SAP HANA and the changes and improvements that it brings, as well as appendices with useful references for the reader.

Throughout the book, there are references to *SAP ERP* (Enterprise Resource Planning) and *SAP ECC* (SAP ERP Central Component). SAP S/4HANA. SAP GTS works best when it is integrated with an ERP program. For the purposes of simplicity, we assume that it is always SAP in this book. It should be noted, however, that SAP GTS can be integrated with non-SAP ERP programs as well.

This book is useful for a wide range of companies at various stages of creating a compliance solution, including:

▶ Companies unfamiliar with international trade compliance requirements that want to increase their knowledge of regulatory guidelines.

▶ Companies evaluating the most appropriate trade compliance solution for them to apply.

▶ Companies committed to GTS that want to understand its functionality better before installation begins.

▶ Companies currently implementing GTS seeking to base their configuration decisions on a solid understanding of their purpose and implications.

▶ Companies using GTS that are considering activating software features not previously used or that want assistance in developing an internal training program.

▶ Companies looking to migrate to the new SAP GTS edition for HANA in order to learn what it entails and what has changed with the new version.

As you can see, this book is intended for multiple audiences at various stages of an implementation project. It is our hope that this book will assist you in your project and lead to a higher level of compliance! However, it must be noted that this book does not offer legal advice. The regulatory compliance discussions are meant to raise awareness; specific answers to your company's questions on regulatory compliance must be directed to your company's legal advisor or expert counsel.

We hope you will find this book as informative and educational as we have found writing it!

We have added a few icons to highlight important information. These include:

> **☞ Tips**
>
> Tips highlight information that provides more details about the subject being described and/or additional background information.

> **! Attention**
>
> Attention notices highlight information that you should be aware of when you go through the examples in this book on your own.

Finally, a note concerning the copyright: all screenshots printed in this book are the copyright of SAP SE. All rights are reserved by SAP SE. Copyright pertains to all SAP images in this publication. For the sake of simplicity, we do not mention this specifically underneath every screenshot.

1 SAP GTS Edition for SAP HANA

SAP's new global trade software on HANA is here. Let's explore what is new and why make the move to global trade edition for HANA.

This version of GTS has been completely redesigned to leverage SAP HANA architecture and the latest innovation in user experience technology. Global Trade Services, edition for HANA is a new product, built entirely on one of the most advanced in-memory platforms. This edition is a result of natural progression to keep up to date with technology and development for over 30 years in SAPs expertise in foreign trade business. Figure 1.1 shows the SAP solution timeline.

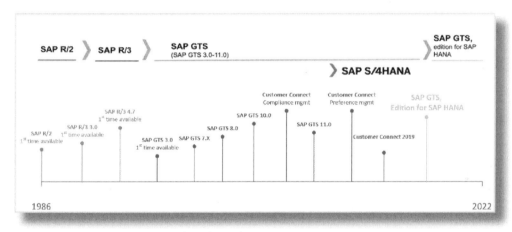

Figure 1.1: International trade and SAP solutions timeline

1.1   SAP Fiori Launchpad

A better user experience with SAP Fiori. The SAP GTS easy access menu that we have all used for decades is replaced by Fiori launchpad. This will be a new and consistent user experience across SAP applications. This latest version of GTS comes with SEVENTEEN newly designed Fiori apps with enhanced usability to increase efficiency and transparency for the users. This also means we are replacing and consolidating over SEVENTY old SAP GUI transactions. Figure 1.2 shows the My Home page view of SAP GTS FIORI dashboard.

13

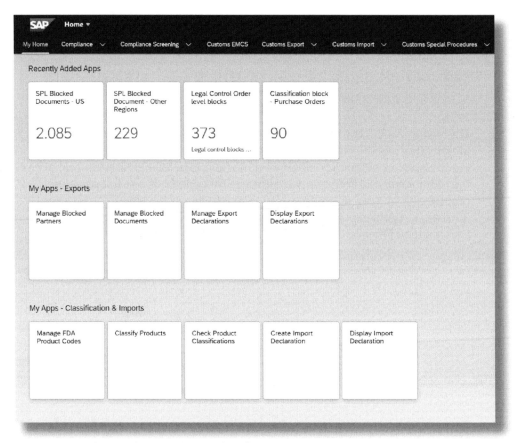

Figure 1.2: New SAP Fiori Launchpad—My Home Page

Improved usability with Native Fiori apps in the following areas of GTS. Figure 1.3 shows some of the new natively built FIORI apps that are delivered as part of the standard release.

- ▶ Trade compliance and screening
  - ▶ Manage blocked partners
  - ▶ Manage blocked documents
  - ▶ Display documents
- ▶ Customs management
  - ▶ Manage and Display Export Declarations, Exit Confirmation and overdue
  - ▶ Manage and Display Transit Declarations, Transit Confirmation and Overdue

- ▶ Trade preference management
  - ▶ Request and Manage LTSD Inbound
  - ▶ Manage LTSD Outbound
  - ▶ Manage Re Issue Reason
  - ▶ Preference Properties for Suppliers
  - ▶ Preference Properties for Customers

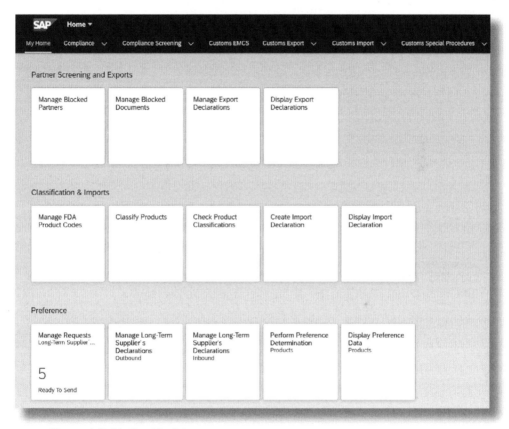

Figure 1.3: Native Fiori Apps

1.2 New Features with Fiori Apps

Natively developed FIORI apps provide built-in analytic capabilities for audits and reporting. Figure 1.4 demonstrates the integrated analytics feature, which displays the number of blocked documents based on different filter parameters. This functionality condenses multiple screens from previous versions into a single comprehensive view. Switching between different legal regulations and the Foreign Trade Organization (FTO) is effortlessly achieved with a simple click of the mouse. Moreover, these analyses can be conveniently shared as links or tiles within the same screen. More details about the FIORI capabilities are discussed in Section 3.11.

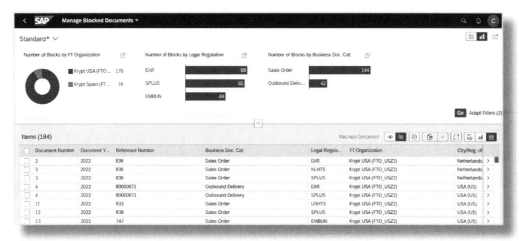

Figure 1.4: Manage blocked documents screen

Screens like export customs declaration (see Figure 1.5 below) also include new concepts of processing status, progress and proposal. Processing status and a detailed view for declaration are easy to read. In addition, filtering and personalizing the display list is easy and efficient.

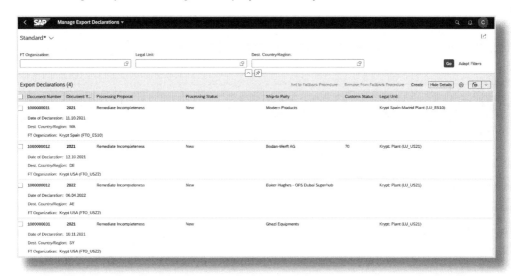

Figure 1.5: Manage export declaration

Using in-built enterprise search capability, it is possible to search selected objects. All matching text will be highlighted. You can search objects, business partner, find export declaration using reference number, SPL entities and so on. Below, Figure 1.6 shows an example of searching for business partner by name.

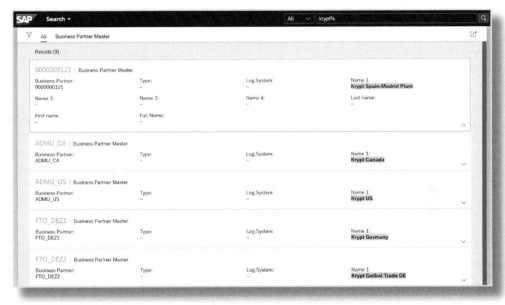

Figure 1.6: Searching for business partner using enterprise search

1.3 Simplifications compared to GTS 11.0

Although SAP GTS edition for HANA comes with additional features and capabilities, it still retains all the reliable and proven functionalities that have been in place for many years. Let's delve into some of these simplified features in SAP GTS edition for HANA.

1.3.1 Compliance Area

TREX engine for SPL screening is no longer supported. New HANA search engine replaces and simplifies the SPL setup.

The screening of HR business partners and applicants is no longer supported in SAP GTS, edition for SAP HANA.

1.3.2   Customs Management

The dashboards for customs management, which used to serve as the entry point for NetWeaver Business Client (NWBC), are no longer available due to the technology on which they were based being deprecated. Unfortunately, there is no substitute provided for these dashboards. As a result, the feature that allowed users to pin export declarations to the pinboards is also no longer functional. Previously, users could do this by clicking on the pin icon located on the left side of the country flag while changing an export declaration.

1.3.3   Trade Preference Management

The handling of *Long-Term supplier declarations (LTSDs)* has undergone a complete revamp. The previous data model has been phased out, along with the associated reports and transactions, and replaced with new reports and Fiori applications.

The exchange of LTSDs via the SAP middleware SAP PI is no longer supported as it was based on the old data model.

The *Pan Euro Med Cumulation Zone* is no longer taken into account when issuing customer-based long-term declarations.

1.3.4   Intrastat

The functionality for excluding regions from Intrastat is available in SAP GTS, but not in SAP GTS, edition for SAP HANA.

The functionality for default values for import worklist is available in SAP GTS, but not in SAP GTS, edition for SAP HANA.

Worklists for Intrastat declarations are available in SAP GTS, but not in SAP GTS edition for SAP HANA.

1.3.5 General changes

Several changes and improvements have been implemented in SAP GTS, edition for SAP HANA. More improvements will be introduced in the upcoming service pack releases as well.

▶ The SAP Easy Access Menu is no longer supported and has been replaced by SAP Fiori Launchpad in SAP GTS, edition for SAP HANA.

▶ The Web Dynpro application and Classification Help are no longer available in SAP GTS, edition for SAP HANA.

▶ Case management for blocked partner and product classification is longer supported in SAP GTS, edition for SAP HANA.

▶ The Application Area Risk Management has been removed and its functions have been reorganized, with Compliance Management and Preference Management now being independent application areas.

▶ Letter of Credit is no longer supported in GTS edition for HANA, but it is now available in S/4 HANA Treasury Management.

1.4 Process Improvements

The new version of GTS edition for HANA improves and updates the way some of the logistics processes integrate with GTS. We will look at all these improvements.

1.4.1 Improved Integration with S/4 HANA TM

Transportation management SAP TM has always had a very tight integration with GTS to share compliance status and to obtain transportation details for customs purposes. This integration was previously limited, but we now have the following improvements:

▶ Enabling *sanctioned party list (SPL)* screening, embargo checks, and legal control checks in freight units

▶ Enabling legal control checks in freight orders

▶ Exchanging customs export relevant information with freight order

▶ Triggering the closure of a customs transit procedure from a freight order

1.4.2 Improvements with S/4 HANA Order to Cash Integration

The order to cash process has always been closely integrated with GTS in order to execute compliance checks. It was always a requirement to have a sneak peak of the GTS status at the sales order level. Now with S/4 HANA this status is in-built at the Sales order line-item level. Now you can see the compliance check results along with the legal control license results. This is achieved through an active push of the compliance status to sales order and scheduling agreement level. See Figure 1.7.

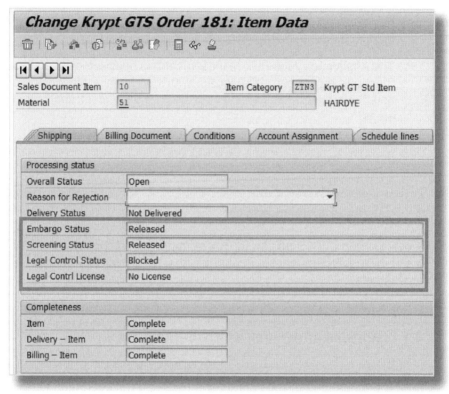

Figure 1.7: S/4 HANA Order Level Status

1.4.3 SAP BW/4HANA Content Add-on

Business Content for SAP BW/4HANA combines the enterprise data warehouse capabilities of SAP BW/4HANA with explorative and interactive real-time analytics using the SAP HANA in-memory database. SAP HANA-optimized Business Content for Global Trade Services supports the analysis of import declaration, export declaration, transit declaration, and transit discharge declaration data. The data is extracted via CDS-Views from Global Trade Services, edition for SAP HANA into SAP BW/4HANA. The following CDS-Views are supplied:

▶ Data Extraction for Export and Import Declaration Items

▶ Data Extraction for Transit Declaration and Discharge Items

▶ Master data CDS view extraction Customs Declaration Type Text and Customs Legal Regulation Text

Note, in order to use SAP BW/4HANA Content, software version 2020 SP02 of SAP Global Trade Services, edition for SAP HANA must be installed.

1.5 Architecture and Integration

The new version of GTS is built on SAP HANA platform 2.0 to leverage the HANA database which allows faster data processing. As we all know, GTS natively interacts with other SAP model and there have been some changes and improvements in the way GTS connects to these applications. Following Figure 1.8 shows the overall connections and latest technology on which the connections are.

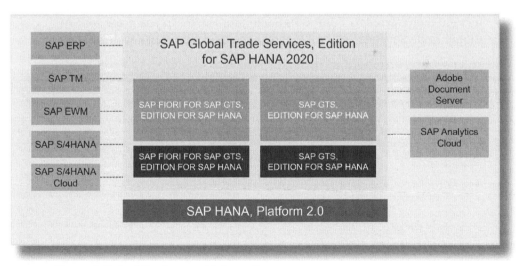

Figure 1.8: Architecture and Integrations

▶ The connection to SAP Transportation Management uses SAP Web Services

▶ The connection to SAP S/4HANA Cloud uses SAP Cloud Connector

▶ The connection to SAP Analytics Cloud uses HTTPS Connection

▶ Embedded or Hub Deployment; Figure 1.8 shows Embedded Deployment

Note: With GTS, edition for HANA 2020 and the use of S/4HANA Foundation, GTS will follow a cycle similar to S/4HANA, but with a release approximately every two years.

1.6 How to keep up with the changes

1.6.1 Road Map explorer

SAP Road Map Explorer can simplify your path to future SAP products and the Intelligent Enterprise. Gain an up-to-date overview on planned and available innovations, as well as technical information, through an interactive road map experience.

How to find it: From sap.com, go to Services & Support, select SAP Road Maps under SAP Help Portal, click on Use the SAP Roadmap Explorer button and then Search for "SAP GTS Edition for HANA" to see plans for SAP Global Trade Services. Figure 1.9 shows the road map explorer view.

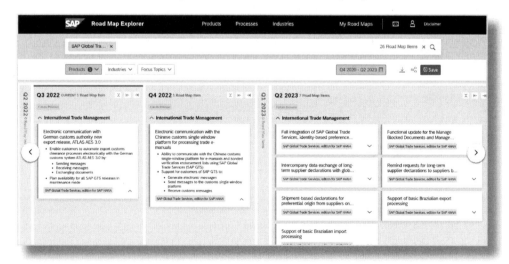

Figure 1.9: SAP Road map explorer to track and plan for new innovations

1.6.2   Legal announcement

With so many legal changes happening around the world SAP GTS edition of HANA will have to stay up to date on those legal changes. These planned or upcoming changes can be easily tracked via one support launchpad. Here you can search for the app "Announcement of Legal Change" and assign the app to your favorites. Figure 1.10 shows the support launchpad view to track legal announcements.

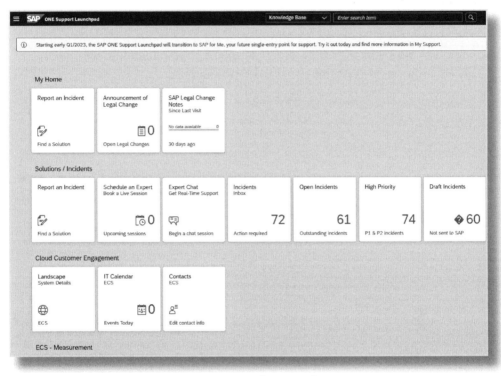

Figure 1.10: Legal announcement notification tile

1.6.3   SAP Help to guide your upgrade

You will find all the required guides and documentation for you to plan for your upgrade. Go to sap.help.com and search for SAP GTS edition for HANA and you will find conversion guides to walk you through the conversion process. This includes following key documentations required for this process.

Conversion guides along with the details of XPRA (Execution of programs after inputs) are available in order to prepare and convert from SAP GTS to GTS Edition for HANA.

Configuration guides describe the settings you need to make to configure the required SAP application components and applications from third parties. The guide does not repeat the descriptions of the individual Customizing activities, but contains specific information about configuring processes in SAP GTS, edition for SAP HANA.

The Integration Guide provides information about configurations and settings that are required for the products that can be integrated with SAP Global Trade Services, edition for SAP HANA.

2 Sanctioned party list screening

One of the most commonly used functions in SAP GTS is *sanctioned party list screening*, or *SPL checking*. SPL checking means that all of your business partners and documents will be checked against known lists of sanctioned or restricted parties. What exactly is a sanctioned/restricted party, and what does it mean for your business?

2.1   Introduction

Everyone understands what a country embargo is; in other words, you may not deal with that country. For example, US companies cannot do business with North Korean companies. However, it is not as well known that government agencies more often embargo individuals and entities than they do countries. For example, the US Department of the Treasury lists entities in certain countries, such as Libya, that it considers a danger to the national interests of the United States. As a result, a US company may not sell to any of the listed companies or individuals. The lists of forbidden or restricted parties are called *Sanctioned Party Lists (SPL)*.

SPL lists are commonly thought of an "export" issue, and most companies understand they must ensure they never export to a listed entity. However, these lists can apply to imports as well as domestic activity. Buying from or selling to a person in your own country could violate certain SPL rules; for example, there are US entities on many of the lists.

It is critical that your business protects itself from liability and screens all of its business partners against the published lists. To do so, a system must be set up that checks *business partners (BP)* as soon as they are created or edited and checks the partners within documents. Any time the system thinks that it has found a match, it will block the partner or document from use until it is reviewed by an authorized user. This user will decide on the block, i.e., is it really a match, or just a close match? If it is simply a close match, they can release the partner/document. If it is a real match, it will remain blocked.

In the next section, we will review the suggested settings, best practices, and user tips for SAP GTS SPL functionality. It is not intended to be exhaustive but rather covers the most commonly used areas of the software, as well as those most likely to cause confusion.

Before we begin, we would like to explain the high-level operation of SAP GTS SPL. To illustrate this, we will look at three simple process flows, including:

▶ How an SPL match is determined.

▶ How a business partner block is determined and managed.

▶ How an order block is determined and managed.

Figure 2.1, Figure 2.2 and Figure 2.3 display these processes in the form of a flow chart. These simple flows are not meant to capture all SAP GTS functionality but rather to provide a high-level overview of its three core competencies: determining a match, blocking a partner that matches, and blocking a document containing a matched partner. For example, there are many more settings available to fine-tune the match logic than what is shown. By reviewing this diagram, you will better be able to understand where the other features fit in and how they affect the outcome of checks.

Let's look at a couple of key terms. When a user reviews a match, they must decide if they are looking at a *true positive* or a *false positive*. A true positive is an actual match, and the business partner is the SPL entity. A false positive means the system found that the two were close enough to warrant a block, but upon review, it has been determined that the match is not real.

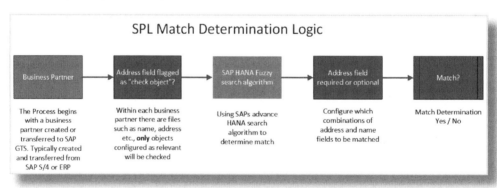

Figure 2.1: SPL Match determination logic

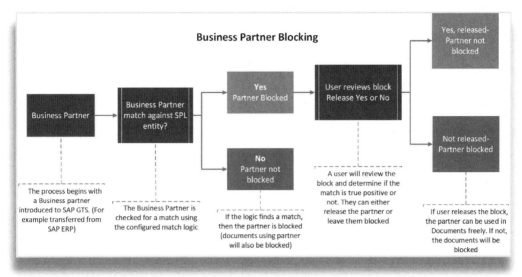

Figure 2.2: SPL Business partner screening flow

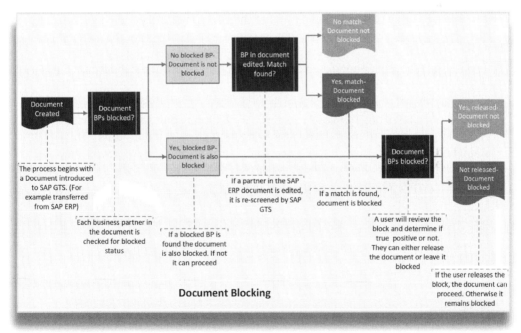

Figure 2.3: Document blocking

This chapter delves into each of these areas in more depth, as well as covering areas not shown in these diagrams. Lastly, it wraps up with a general discussion on SPL compliance and tips for meeting the expected compliance standard.

2.2 SAP HANA Search Overview

SAP HANA search is a robust search feature that delivers speed and fault tolerance, providing an efficient and reliable solution to businesses. It covers the majority of functionalities found in SAP GTS search and SAP TREX search, making it a powerful tool for searching through large amounts of data. With SAP HANA search, businesses can experience a range of benefits, including improved performance, simplified SPL setup, and a streamlined SPL screening process.

One of the significant advantages of using SAP HANA search is the *performance improvement* it offers. With its in-memory database system, SAP HANA enables users to process large amounts of data in real-time, allowing for faster and more efficient search results. This can be especially beneficial for businesses that need to search through vast amounts of data quickly and accurately.

Another benefit of SAP HANA search is the *simplified SPL setup*. The system makes it easy to set up and configure the search feature, enabling businesses to begin using it with minimal hassle. The simplified setup process ensures that businesses can implement SAP HANA search quickly and efficiently, reducing the need for extensive IT support and troubleshooting.

Finally, SAP HANA search also offers a *streamlined SPL screening* process. The system allows businesses to screen transactions against multiple lists, ensuring that they remain compliant with regulatory requirements. This simplified screening process reduces the risk of errors and improves the overall efficiency of the screening process, enabling businesses to meet their compliance obligations more effectively.

SAP GTS Edition for HANA now supports two options for SPL Screening:

▶ Classic SPL algorithm within SAP GTS ("SAP GTS Search")

▶ SAP HANA Search

> **☛ Note**
>
> In this book we will see all the settings and details about SAP HANA search option. We will also highlight any standard configuration that is applicable for traditional SAP GTS Search and not applicable for SAP HANA Search

2.3 Configuration—SPL HANA Search

SPL screening involves screening your business partner (BP) against lists of SPL uploaded to SAP GTS as XML files. Third party companies provide this content as a service and send out updates when the government updates the list. SPL involves screening text or characters, which is very performance intensive. To address this, SAP GTS allows the user to build an index of denied party list (SPL) content using the latest SAP HANA Search. Business partners use this index to improve screening performance.

SAP GTS provides many options and flexibility for SPL Screening. It can adjust to match the business needs of any organization based on its risk exposure and business activity. This sort of flexibility is available through multiple settings from which each installation can choose. There are two key areas of configuration that determine these settings: (a) control settings, which influence the way SPL functionality functions, and (b) control procedures, which allow certain rules to be set within user control, such as exclusion, alias, etc.

All of the content and screens shown in Section 2.2 are configured and accessed through the following menu path: SPRO • SAP REFERENCE IMG • SAP GLOBAL TRADE SERVICES, EDITION FOR SAP HANA • COMPLIANCE MANAGEMENT • SANCTIONED PARTY LIST SCREENING SERVICE.

2.3.1 Control settings

To maximize the comparison index effectiveness, it is important that you ensure that the SPL controls for the index are set correctly. Use transaction SPRO or follow menu path SAP REFERENCE IMG • SAP GLOBAL TRADE SERVICES, EDITION FOR SAP HANA • COMPLIANCE MANAGEMENT • SANCTIONED PARTY LIST SCREENING SERVICE • CONTROL SETTINGS FOR SANCTIONED PARTY LIST SCREENING.

Once in the CONTROL SETTINGS area, highlight the SPL Legal Regulation (i. e., SPLUS) and click on DETAILS 🔍. Let's review the key sections in this area.

Scope of check

In the CONSIDER VALIDITY field, select the third option from the drop-down menu INCLUDE BOTH VALID FROM AND VALID TO DATE (see Figure 2.4). This validity check keeps track of SPL entries that drop off the SPL list. This selection notes whether you want to see matches against expired SPL entities (i.e., do you want to know if your customer used to be on an SPL list?).

> **☛ Adjust technical validity of SPL entities:**
>
> When using valid from and valid to option make sure the SPL entities validities are adjusted. This should happen automatically, but you can make sure by running the FIORI APP "Adjust Technical validity in Accordance with Official Validity" or T-code "/SAPSLL/SPL_MD05" in SAP GUI for SPL legal regulation 'SPLUS'

If you have a business partner with multiple addresses, select the MULTIPLE ADDRESS CHECK ACTIVE check box.

If you want expired records to be marked for deletion, you can check the SET DELETION INDICATOR ACCORDING TO OFFICIAL VALIDITY check box.

CHECK LOGIC FOR DOCS: Maintain the default setting STATUS CHECK OF UNCHANGED ADDRESSES (PARTNER ADDRESS). This ensures that all document partner addresses are checked. A status check is performed for unchanged partner addresses. Screening is performed for only manually changed partner addresses.

SEARCH STRATEGY: This option is not applicable for SPL HANA search option.

SIZE OF CHECK PACKAGE: Maintain this size based on performance testing and sizing. For volume transfer, we normally recommend keeping the size between 50,000 and 100,000 for performance reasons. Of course, you must decide if this works for your total number of partners.

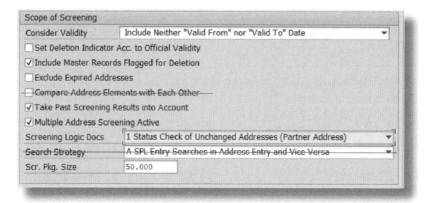

Figure 2.4: SPL scope of check setup

System control

System control setup for storing comparison index and the Time Initialized option (see Figure 2.5) is not applicable for SPL HANA search and it is only required if you switch to traditional "GTS Search Algorithm."

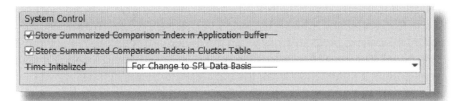

Figure 2.5: System control settings not applicable for HANA Search

Audit

SPL Audit recording for the four different screening scenarios in SAP GTS has the following THREE options. It can be set according to your business needs for each of the screening scenario. See Figure 2.6

- ▶ ' '—NEVER WRITE AUDIT—Never log the screening results
- ▶ 'X'—ALWAYS WRITE AUDIT—Always log the screening results
- ▶ 'Y'—WRITE AUDIT FOR SPL HITS FOUND OR NEGATIVE STATUS CHECK— Log the screening results for only real SPL hits or Negative Status Check

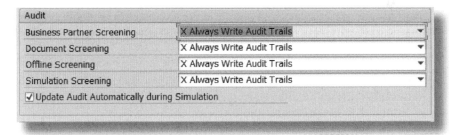

Figure 2.6: SPL Audit Options

In order to improve performance and save transfer time, we recommend that you set all AUDIT options to BLANK during the initial conversion (i.e., when the production system is set up, but prior to go-live when the data is mass transferred), if you have a large volume of business partner records. Writing to the audit trail takes additional processing time, and the business partner conversion might run for hours. Once the business partner records are transferred, the audit trail recording option can be activated.

Notification

SPL configuration allows you to send a notification if documents are blocked due to SPL screening. Check the SEND MAIL WHEN DOCUMENT BLOCKED option if you want to send an email when the document is blocked (see Figure 2.7). Check the SEND MAIL WHEN BUSINESS PARTNER BLOCKED option if you want to send a notification when the business partner is blocked.

Figure 2.7: Notification settings

Note that there is still work to be done in BASIS before this functionality will work. Set up the prerequisite steps that are part of the SAP GTS workflow settings:

1. To maintain user groups, use FIORI APP MAINTAIN USER GROUP. These help group the users to whom you would like to send the notification.

2. To activate email notification for blocked documents, use FIORI APP NOTIFICATION CONTROL FOR BLOCKED DOCUMENTS, to maintain the foreign trade organization, legal regulation (e. g., SPLUS), and user groups that were maintained in step #1.

3. To active email notification for blocked partners, use FIORI APP NOTIFICATION CONTROL FOR BLOCKED PARTNERS to maintain the foreign trade organization, legal regulation (e. g., SPLUS), and user groups that were maintained in the previous step #1.

We will return to CONTROL SETTINGS shortly, but first it makes sense to discuss the CONTROL PROCEDURE.

Additional settings for SPL Screening

Follow menu path SAP REFERENCE IMG • SAP GLOBAL TRADE SERVICES • SAP COMPLIANCE MANAGEMENT • SANCTIONED PARTY LIST SCREENING SERVICE •

CONTROL SETTINGS FOR SANCTIONED PARTY LIST SCREENING to return to the control settings highlighted in Figure 2.8.

Note: List types shown are property of Descartes (MK Denial) and used with permission

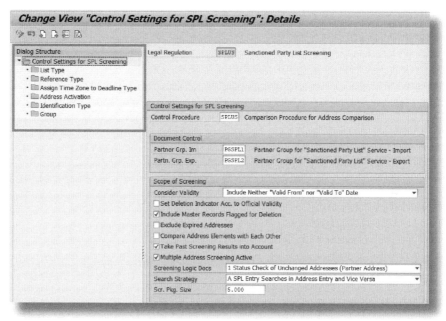

Figure 2.8: Additional settings for SPL screening

List types

The first task is to set up and review the LIST TYPES.

> **! List types**
>
> We highly recommended that you use a subscription provider for your SPL list content. SPL lists are large and change rapidly. Attempting to maintain them manually is risky and will take a great deal of time and effort. Subscription providers are available that will offer you this content, which is regularly updated, for a reasonable price. The example used in this book is Descartes (MK Denial), which offers comprehensive SPL data for GTS users. See Section 2.5 for further discussion on subscription services.

With SPL HANA all that is required is the search option defining the list types. The configuration available at each list type to define minimum and maximum length is no longer required and its applicable only if you select the "GTS Search" Option. If you are using a subscription service and do not want to make any changes, you can move on to reference type. See Figure 2.9.

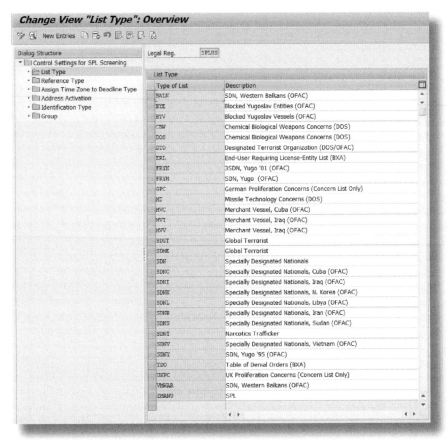

Figure 2.9: List types configuration settings

Reference type

In the control setting configuration step, click the REFERENCE TYPE folder to bring up the details shown in Figure 2.10. Reference types are a way to ensure accurate reading of acronyms in names. For example, if the business partner was "SAP A.K.A. SAP AG" and the SPL was "SAP (Also Known As SAP AG)," this match may be missed because of the significant difference in the names. Capturing A.K.A. as shown in Figure 2.10 ensures that it will not be missed. Some data subscription providers will also provide suggested reference type data that can be populated automatically.

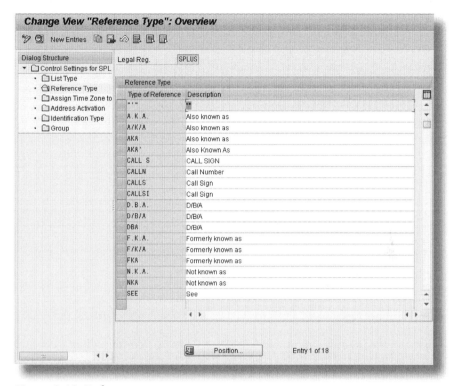

Figure 2.10: Reference types

Assign time zone

Click ASSIGN TIME ZONE in the DEADLINE TYPE folder to bring up the screen shown in Figure 2.11. A specific time zone can be assigned that will be considered when "to" and "from" dates are relevant to an SPL search.

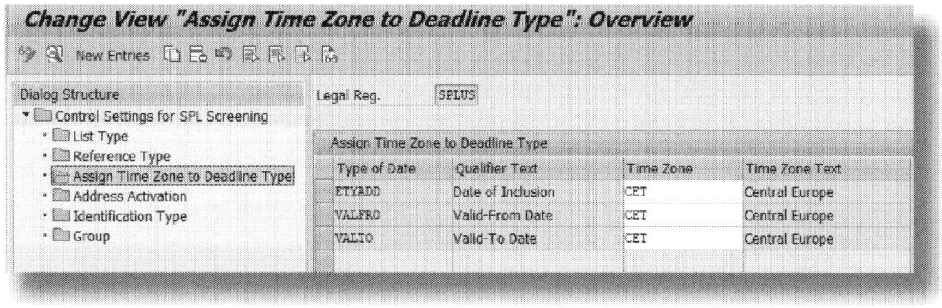

Figure 2.11: Assign time zone

Address activation

Click on the ADDRESS ACTIVATION folder to bring up the details screen shown in Figure 2.12. The system delivered address is the STANDARD ADDRESS; any other preferred address type can be added to the screen.

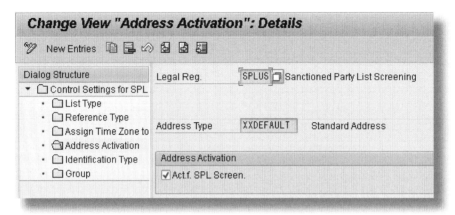

Figure 2.12: Activate address types

Identification Type

Click on the Identification type folder to define identification that are screened as part of the SPL screening. The following are some commonly used identification types:

Passport: This identification type can be used to identify individuals in the SPL. It includes information such as the passport number, country of issue, and expiration date.

National ID: This identification type can be used to identify individuals in the SPL. It includes information such as the national identification number, country of issue, and expiration date.

DUN: This identification type stands for "Data Universal Numbering System" and is a unique nine-digit number that is assigned to each business location by Dun & Bradstreet. It can be used to identify a party in the SPL.

EIN: This identification type stands for "Employer Identification Number" and is a unique nine-digit number assigned to businesses by the Internal Revenue Service (IRS) in the United States. It can be used to identify a party in the SPL.

TIN: This identification type stands for "Tax Identification Number" and is a unique identification number assigned to each taxpayer by the tax authorities in a country. It can be used to identify a party in the SPL.

2.3.2 Activate the business partner at the business partner function level

Follow menu path SAP REFERENCE IMG • SAP GLOBAL TRADE SERVICES, EDITION FOR SAP HANA • SAP COMPLIANCE MANAGEMENT • SANCTIONED PARTY LIST SCREENING SERVICE • ACTIVATE BUSINESS PARTNER AT BUSINESS PARTNER FUNCTION LEVEL (see Figure 2.13).

Change View "Business Partner: Control Settings": Overview

New Entries

Business Partner: Control Settings

ApplObj	BP Role	Block Type	SPL Time
BUPA	BUP001	1 Process is interrupted - .. ▼	1 Synchronous - When Obj ▲
BUPA	BUP003	1 Process is interrupted - .. ▼	1 Synchronous - When Obj ▼
BUPA	SLLCPC	1 Process is interrupted - .. ▼	1 Synchronous - When Obj
BUPA	SLLCPS	1 Process is interrupted - .. ▼	1 Synchronous - When Obj

Figure 2.13: Type of SPL block

This task involves setting up the application object control settings for business partners and their associated business partner functions. The control settings involve selecting the type of SPL BLOCK (the default setting is titled 1 PROCESS IS INTERRUPTED—SYSTEM REMOVES BLOCK), the time of the SPL check (ASYNCHRONOUS—WHEN OBJECT IS UPDATED), and the business area it falls under (Logistics, Financial Accounting, or Human Resources). From here, you can highlight one of the lines and click on the DETAILS button (see Figure 2.14).

Change View "Business Partner: Control Settings": Details

New Entries

| Application Object | BUPA |
| Partner Function | SLLCPC   Global Trade Services: Business Partner (Customer) |

Business Partner: Control Settings

Type of SPL Block	1 Process is interrupted - system removes block
Time of SPL Check	1 Synchronous - When Object Is Updated
Sep. Bus. Areas	A0 Logistics

☐ Enhanced Authorization Check in Sanctioned Party List Screening Area

Figure 2.14: Business partner screening control settings

The default SPL block setting means that the system screens the business partner. If it finds a block based on the system parameter settings, it blocks this business partner. Users can then review the results and manually release the block or take appropriate action. For the TIME OF SPL CHECK field, we recommend that you use SYNCHRONOUS, except during conversion or volume transfer, when it should be set to ASYNCHRONOUS. Then revert back to SYNCHRONOUS for ongoing or regular transfers.

The separation into business area (SEP. BUS. AREAS) field ensures that blocked business partners and associated transactions fall under the appropriate view for operational effectiveness and reporting. Settings are pre-delivered for customers and vendors, but you must ensure that the entries for other business partner roles (e.g., contact person, employee, or bank) are maintained. To restrict the control of review of business partners by company codes within your organization, select the check box ENHANCED AUTHORIZATION CHECK in the SANCTIONED PARTY LIST SCREENING AREA and ensure that the security profile has the FOREIGN TRADE ORGANIZATION checkbox selected.

2.3.3   Activate legal regulations

The SPL Legal Regulation must be activated in order to function. The parameter can be set for this activation, which can be country or a combination of country and country group (for example–you could specifically name the USA or make a group containing the USA and Canada). For this example, we will set up the activation by country, but the same process would apply if you choose to make country groups. The decision should be made based on how many countries are being dealt with—if it is a small number, individual country makes sense. If there are dozens of countries, it may be appropriate to use groups to save time and effort (see Figure 2.15 for an example).

Legal regulations allow the definition of the configuration within the system specific to the function (SPL, License determination, or customs declaration) within SAP GTS. To activate the SPL legal regulation by each country, there are five different options to choose from:

1. Check: Dispatch (exclusively)

2. Check: Export (exclusively)

3. Check: Dispatch/Export (excluding domestic)

4. Check: Dispatch/Export (including domestic)

5. No check (no SPL service activation)

Figure 2.15: Country-level activation

We highly recommended that you choose option four, which will ensure that your domestic partners and transactions are screened, as well as your imports/exports. Many SPL lists apply domestically as well as during export. If a narrower selection is required for a business reason (e.g., to reduce the number of false positive hits), be mindful to ensure that it is compliant. Consider making multiple legal regulations so that domestic screening can be performed on the critical lists, and export only screening on the less sensitive ones. For a more detailed discussion of these lists, see Section 2.10.1.

2.3.4 Define reasons for releasing blocked documents and business partners

There is an optional feature in GTS that allows a *reason for release to be assigned*. This feature allows the user to specify why they released a partner during their review. We recommended that you use this feature as outlined in the steps below. Adding reasons at the time of release will increase the value of the audit trail should any decisions be questioned at a later point in time.

The menu path is SAP REFERENCE IMG • SAP GLOBAL TRADE SERVICES, EDITION FOR SAP HANA • SAP COMPLIANCE MANAGEMENT • DEFINE REASONS FOR RELEASING BLOCKED DOCUMENTS AND BUSINESS PARTNERS.

In this screen, you can enter a NEW ENTRY, or pull up the list of current entries by choosing OPTIONS FOR RELEASE REASON. Current options can be edited and/or deleted. Figure 2.16 is an example of a list of reasons. Each business must choose its own reasons, and this is intended only as an example to provide some ideas. GTS does not come loaded with reasons, and they must be set up if they are to be used. Release reasons will be helpful for reporting and analyzing the trend of SPL hits present in the system.

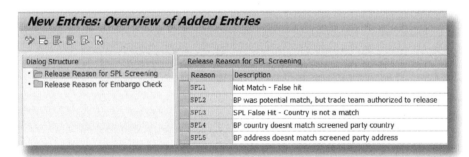

Figure 2.16: Release reasons

2.4 GTS SPL HANA Search

Another important control within the configuration is the control procedure to compare addresses. This configuration is in menu path SAP REFERENCE IMG • SAP GLOBAL TRADE SERVICES, EDITION FOR SAP HANA • SAP COMPLIANCE MANAGEMENT • SANCTIONED PARTY LIST SCREENING SERVICE • DEFINE COMPARISON PROCEDURE FOR ADDRESS COMPARISON. See below Figure 2.17.

Provide a description for the comparison procedure and maintain the main language of data to be considered; this will typically be "EN".

In this section you will be able to choose your search algorithm as *SAP HANA Search.*

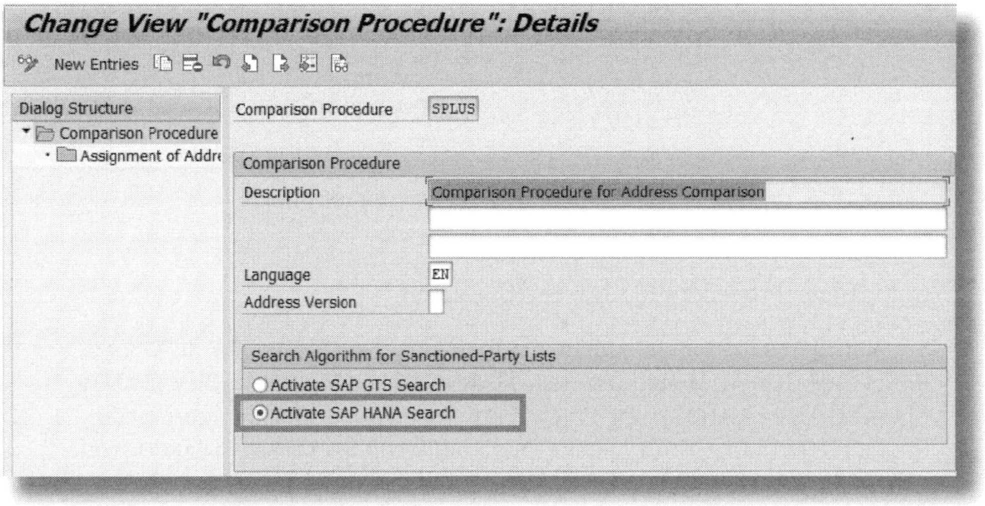

Figure 2.17: Define Comparison Procedure

Assign address fields

Click THE ASSIGN ADDRESS FIELDS folder to bring up the screen in Figure 2.18. You can see the delivered fields for SPL screening. Click the NEW ENTRIES button to add fields that you want to screen (e. g., CITY2).

This is referring to the fields from your SAP ERP Central Component (SAP ECC) system in the business partner master. There are typically multiple fields for a field category such as "Name."

You can choose to review all of the available fields for a category, such as reviewing "Name 1" through "Name 4." If you have reason to believe there is corrupt data in some of these fields, you may want to reduce the fields reviewed. For example, you could choose to look only at "Name 1" and "Name 2."

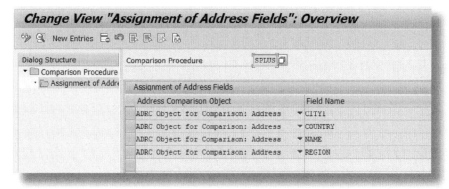

Figure 2.18: Comparison procedure with assign address fields

Comparison Procedure for SAP HANA Search

You can define the comparison in the following menu path: SAP REFERENCE IMG · SAP GLOBAL TRADE SERVICES, EDITION FOR SAP HANA · COMPLIANCE MANAGEMENT · SANCTIONED PARTY LIST SCREENING · DEFINE COMPARISON PROCEDURE · DEFINE COMPARISON PROCEDURE FOR SAP HANA SEARCH. You can set up rules relevant to SAP HANA search algorithm to carry out sanctioned party list (SPL) screening. See Figure 2.19.

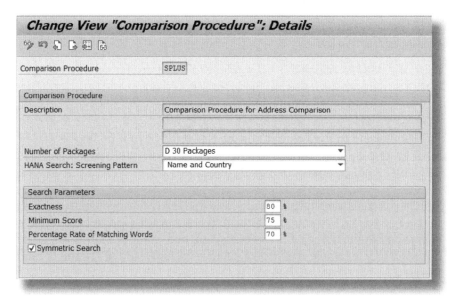

Figure 2.19: SAP HANA Search Comparison Procedure

NUMBER OF PACKAGES—To optimize system performance of SAP HANA Search, you can select a suitable number of packages that SAP HANA Search should execute in parallel in multi-core processors, depending on the hardware configuration. SAP offers Package size 1 through 30. Generally, we recommend selecting option D with 30 packages to get the best performance based on project implementations.

SCREENING PATTERN—This search parameter defines which address elements SAP HANA Search checks. SAP offers following six default search patterns:

▶ NAME AND COUNTRY—To get a hit, both the name and country in the addresses must match against the respective elements in the sanctioned-party lists.

▶ NAME ONLY—To get a hit, only the name in the addresses must match against the respective elements in the sanctioned-party lists.

▶ NAME, COUNTRY, AND STREET ADDRESS—To get a hit, the name, country and street in the addresses must match against the respective elements in the sanctioned-party lists.

▶ NAME, COUNTRY, CITY, AND STREET ADDRESS—To get a hit, the name, country, city and street in the addresses must match against the respective elements in the sanctioned-party lists.

▶ NAME OR ADDRESS ELEMENTS STREET, CITY AND COUNTRY—To get a hit, the name or the combination of country, city and street in the addresses must match against the respective elements in the sanctioned-party lists.

▶ NAME AND COUNTRY OR ADDRESS ELEMENTS STREET, CITY AND COUNTRY—To get a hit, the combination of name and country or the combination of country, city and street in the addresses must match against the respective elements in the sanctioned-party lists.

EXACTNESS—This is the parameter in SPL HANA search that measures the degree of similarity between two words. It is represented by a percentage between 0 and 100, with higher values indicating a greater degree of similarity required for a match. This is based on the fuzzy(X) predicate.

It is important to find the right balance in setting the exactness value. A higher exactness value may result in missing out on real hits, while a lower value may lead to a large number of false positives.

43

☞ **Recommended value for "Exactness"**

The recommended value for "Exactness" is between **75% and 82%.**

Following Figure 2.20 explains the relationship between SPL index and BP Index fuzzy score. The example SPL Index words One, Two and Three are compared to the BP Index words terms Won, Zwo and Tree.

SPL Index \ BP Index	WON	ZWO	TREE
ONE	0.61		
TWO	0.61	0.61	
THREE			0.81

Figure 2.20: Example to explain the fuzzy logic and exactness score

MINIMUM SCORE—The minimum score is a number between 0 and 100 that specifies how precise two names or two addresses must match to be considered as a hit. The searched address may contain more than one index. Each index is compared to the threshold, referred to as search parameter 'Exactness', which defines the minimum score a single index must reach. The overall score differs from the similarity score of a single index, it is computed out of the similarity scores of matching indexes and other influences of search parameters such as stop words, term mappings, etc.

☞ **Recommended value range for "minimum score"**

The recommended value range for "minimum score" is between **78% and 81%.**

PERCENTAGE RATE OF MATCHING WORDS—The "Percentage Rate of Matching Words" defines the proportion of matching indexes in a business partner or document partner address. A match is recognized if the number of matching indexes is equal to or greater than the value specified for this search parameter, divided by the total number of indexes in the business partner or document partner's address.

Based on our experience, a high percentage rate of matching words can increase the risk of missing true hits. Therefore, it is recommended that a value of 66% be used. However, if less significant indexes (e.g. "Ltd." and others) can be identified and added to stop words, the percentage rate of matching words can be increased to between $70-75\%$.

> 👉 **Recommended value range for "Percentage Rate"**
>
> The recommended value range for "Percentage Rate" is between **70% and 75%**.

SYMMETRIC SEARCH—The default approach used by the system to calculate the matching percentage rate is based on the number of indexes in the business partner or document partner addresses. However, the "Symmetric Search" parameter provides an option to activate symmetric AND comparison, which considers the number of indexes in the sanctioned-party list as well.

> 👉 **Activate the symmetric search**
>
> The recommendation is to **activate** the symmetric search.

General Settings

There are few SPL HANA parameters that can be maintained by SPL super users directly in the system without going through the configuration. This is provided in order to fine-tune and maintain the parameters as required. These settings can be accessed by FIORI APP DEFINE COMPARISON PROCEDURE FOR SAP HANA. See Figure 2.21.

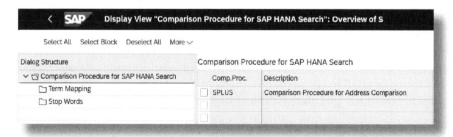

Figure 2.21: General Settings—Comparison Procedure SPL HANA

TERM MAPPINGS—This is a useful tool for expanding search capabilities by adding additional search terms to user input. When a user enters a search term, the term is expanded to include synonyms, hypernyms, hyponyms, and other related terms. This can result in additional records or documents being returned to the user that may be relevant to their search.

Term mappings work by defining a unidirectional replacement, where one term is replaced with another. For example, if 'Limited' is defined as mapping to 'LTD', then 'Limited' will be replaced with 'LTD', but not the other way around. This is particularly helpful when searching with hypernyms, as it allows all hyponyms to be found without returning irrelevant results. However, for bidirectional replacements such as synonyms, both directions need to be added to the term mapping in order to function correctly.

STOPWORDS—Stopwords refer to terms that are deemed less significant for a search and are therefore excluded from generating the result set. This means that the search is conducted as if the stopwords were not present in both the user input and the database column.

However, stopwords do have an impact on the score that is calculated. A record with stopwords that match the user input exactly will receive a higher score compared to a record with missing or differing stopwords. Stopwords can be defined as single terms or as stopword phrases consisting of multiple terms. Stopword phrases are only applied when all terms of the stopword appear in the exact order given.

Operation Simplification

The most important change to the user process with HANA and SPL is when SPL data is updated. Most installations of GTS have subscription-based content for SPL. This means the lists are constantly being updated and changed. With traditional SAP GTS, after each content change, there was a complicated set of master data updates that had to be managed to rebuild indexes.

Similarly, any time the business partner data was updated, the comparison terms needed to be recreated. Unlike the traditional SPL search, HANA search optimizes this part of the operation and eliminates the need for those extra steps. As you can see in Figure 2.22, four steps are no longer needed when you update SPL content, and two steps are no longer needed when you change business partners. When you change SPL configuration settings, you can adjust the SPL general settings by adding new stopwords etc., and you don't need to perform any other step before immediately running the SPL screening with new settings. This is ideal for doing what-if analysis by changing various parameters.

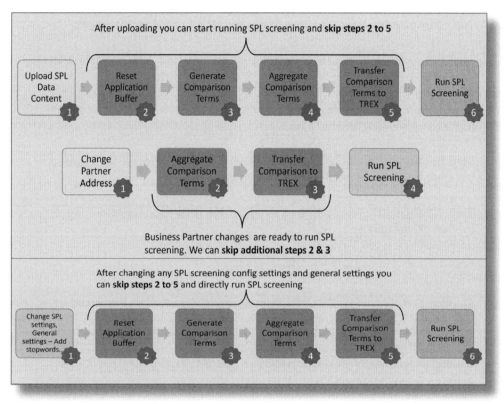

Figure 2.22: Simplified HANA Process

HANA Search Optimization via standard BAdI

SAP has provided two options to optimize the HANA search if the standard configurations do not meet the business criteria.

1. BAdI: /SAPSLL/SPL_HANA_SEARCH **Define Number of Packages for Mass Search Using SAP HANA**

The Customizing activity available for a number of packages under SAP HANA Search—Define Comparison Procedure, is designed to divide large sets of business partner or document partner addresses into smaller packages, which are then allocated across multiple processors in the system based on the "Number of Packages" setting. If the default configuration is not enough for the system's hardware setup, the BAdI (Business Add-In) can be used to increase the number of packages and improve system performance.

The following steps describe how to increase the number of packages:

Step 1: Use ABAP in Eclipse to create your own ABAP class by duplicating the existing "/SAPSLL/CL_SPL_HANA_SEARCH" ABAP Class.

Step 2: Replace all instances of "/SAPSLL/CL_SPL_HANA_SEARCH" with the name of your newly created class.

Step 3: Override the public method "SCREEN_MASS_ADDRESSES" by copying the code from the private method "MASS_SCREEN_D".

Step 4: Modify the relevant code to adjust the package size and improve system performance.

Step 5: Save and activate your ABAP class.

2. BAdI: /SAPSLL/SPL_CMPCT **Override Standard Comparison Procedure**

We can define SPL screening thresholds in a comparison procedure by configuring different control settings. It is important to note that each comparison procedure is only applicable to a specific legal regulation. It is not easy to create and maintain multiple legal regulations for SPL screening. In those cases, the standard comparison procedure can be overridden for a particular SPL screening scenario by utilizing this BAdI (Business Add-In) to dynamically choose a comparison scenario that best suits the business needs.

Method GET_CMPCT—Implement the method to override the standard comparison procedure that is assigned to the given legal regulation and SPL screening scenario.

Import Parameters: IS_SPL_SCEN_ATTR—SPL screening scenario and object attributes. You can use the scenario to choose different comparison procedures.

Export Parameters: ES_SPL_SCEN_CMPCT—SPL screening scenario that is based on a legal regulation.

The following are the supported scenarios:

A1 Address changed—business partner master

A2 Address changed—document

B1 Periodic rescreening—business partner master

B2 Periodic rescreening—document

C1 SPL data basis changed—business partner master

C2 SPL data basis changed—document

S1 Simulation—business partner master

S2 Simulation—document

S3 Simulation—independent address

O3 Offline—independent address

2.5 Subscription service

We highly recommended that you subscribe to a data provider for your SPL lists. The lists are not static and can have additions or deletions on a daily basis. Considering the many lists in play and the fact that each can change on any given day, it is essential that you receive these lists from a third party. There are reputable third parties that make it their business to monitor the various SPL lists and ensure that the data feed is up to date.

There are three key decisions you must make regarding your subscription:

1. Choose a data provider.

2. Select specific subscription lists from those available.

3. Maintain subscription lists.

2.5.1 Choose a data provider

There are multiple options for SPL content, and we encourage you to seek out the option that makes the most sense for your business. Review the following sections to help you make your decision and compare service provider offerings to your business needs. In addition, ensure that they offer the data in an SAP GTS ready format.

For the purposes of demonstration in this book, all of the screenshots with content and list names are from Descartes (MK Denial), and are used with permission. For more information about Descartes (MK Denial), please see:

https://www. descartes.com/resources/knowledge-center/Descartes-MKDenial-Denied-Parties-Screening-data

2.5.2   Selecting specific subscription lists

Most third parties offer a selection of lists you can subscribe to. You need to decide which lists you require and ensure that they are included. The provider may offer individual lists to choose from or may offer a bundle of lists. Either way, make sure the lists you need are included in the agreement you make. If there is any doubt about your requirements, get outside help to assist you, such as a trade compliance consultant.

You will find a more detailed discussion in the compliance tips provided in Appendix 1: SPL list types and references, which also provides a table of commonly used SPL lists and their abbreviations.

2.5.3   Maintenance of subscription lists

However, having a subscription service is not enough. You also need to ensure two things:

1. Daily updates to the SPL data as changes/additions are sent to you by your subscription provider.

2. A strategy for screening all of your previously released business partners against the daily changes.

Daily updates

The various sanctioned party lists are subject to change at any time and may have daily additions/modifications when the global political climate demands it. The government uses many of these lists as economic sanctions, designed to deter the behavior of another country, or perhaps stop the activities of a non-country-based organization (such as drug cartels or terrorists). When global events demand a rapid response, the US government can add new entities daily as members of these groups are identified.

Sticking with US government lists as examples, you are expected to restrict activity with the listed party the day they are publicly listed (such as through a notice in the Federal Register). For example, imagine you have a customer you have dealt with for years and had no reason to suspect them of illegal activity. Unfortunately, they are in fact part of a drug cartel, and the costs/profits from their business are a way for the drug kingpins to launder their drug proceeds. The DEA realizes this, and your customer is listed as a sanctioned party under the Department of the Treasury OFAC rules.

> ### ! You need to ask yourself:
> Does your business have the responsiveness to react to SPL list changes immediately? Imagine that the President just listed someone by Executive Order today. Will the order you have on the books that is shipping tomorrow to this customer be blocked?

To ensure this, you must work with your SPL data provider and ensure that they are giving you daily updates and that you are plugging those into your GTS system daily. Typically, data providers will feed you the updates through a web portal or an FTP site. This will not automatically load the change to SAP GTS; you must ensure that a system is in place to do so. Failing to be responsive could be a fatal weakness in your SPL compliance strategy.

Rescreening previously released partners (delta screenings)

Another critical action related to the daily updates is rescreening your existing customer base against the updates/additions. When you update the SPL data with the new data from your provider, this only ensures that future screenings will include this new, updated data. What about your previously screened partners? Keeping with our example from above, for the customer that is now a listed OFAC sanctioned party, what will block the delivery?

It is important to understand how SAP GTS manages screened partners and documents to make this clear. Figure 2.23 demonstrates how SAP handles a previously screened partner and any documents using that partner.

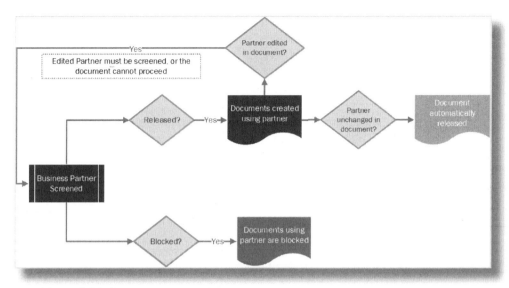

Figure 2.23: Document screening process

Once a Business Partner (BP) is released, provided it is never edited, it can be used in documents going forward without a block. Furthermore, as long as that document does not edit the partner at all, it will not even be screened (because the system notes that the partner has already been screened and released). Staying with our example, we could have a problem if the BP was added subsequently to an SPL list after its release. This situation is illustrated in Figure 2.24.

As you can see in our example, even though we updated our SPL data, our existing customer will still be processed on a sales order without a block. How should you deal with this? You need to run delta screenings daily if you want maximum compliance and protection. A *delta screening* screens **all** of your previously released partners against the changed/updated SPL. It will only screen against SPL entries that are new or changed, since the BP was already screened against all the other SPL data previously.

In our example, this would cause our BP to be blocked since it would be screened against the new SPL data, which includes the OFAC list they were just added to. This also ensures documents using that BP will be blocked.

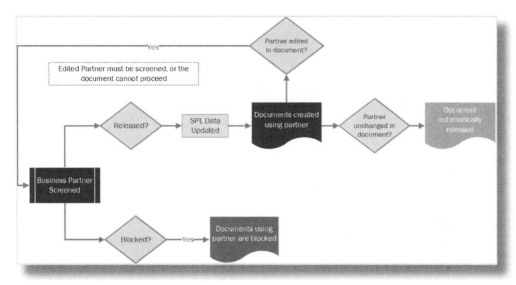

Figure 2.24: Document screening process with newly listed entity

Performing daily updates and delta screenings ensures the highest level of compliance and protection.

2.6 Block alerts

SAP GTS block alerts can be notified to users in several ways.

- ▶ Email Alerts—You can configure an email to be sent out on order blocks in GTS
- ▶ You can notify the order blocks via a pop-up when creating the order in the ERP system
- ▶ Users can view the order status tab to view the SAP GTS screening status

When you configure SAP GTS, you can set it so that users are warned when they create a partner or document that is blocked. Typically, the primary SAP S/4 HANA (we will assume SAP S/4 HANA is integrated to GTS) will display a warning message to the SAP user as displayed in Figure 2.25.

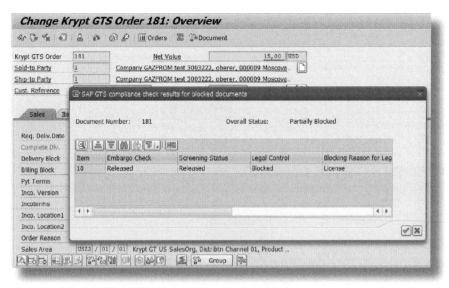

Figure 2.25: S/4 ERP GTS block pop-up on order save

The example in Figure 2.25 is the warning message that appears when a customer service agent enters a new sales order and GTS finds a potential match resulting in a blocked document. This pop-up message display can be controlled by configuring for which orders these pop-ups should be displayed.

SAP GTS also has the functionality to email users when it blocks a document or a business partner. This is important because the user who caused the block (e. g., by entering the order) is usually not the same user who will review/release the block. You will want these emails to go directly to the individual or group responsible for review/release of GTS blocks. See Section 2.3.1 Notification for setup instructions.

SAP GTS screening results are automatically saved in the order status tab in S/4 HANA sales order line level. See Figure 2.26.

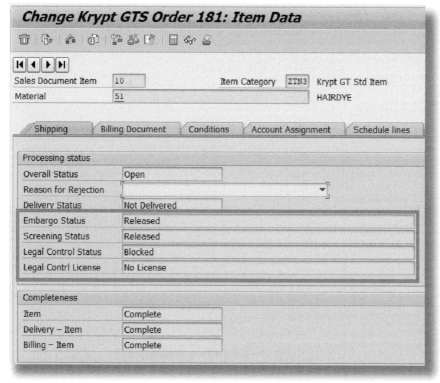

Figure 2.26: SAP GTS screening status in S/4 HANA

Please see Section 2.10 of this chapter for additional compliance tips information and a suggested release/notification strategy.

2.7 Logistics—daily execution

The SPL functions required for daily execution can be found UNDER COM-PLIANCE SCREENING—OVERVIEW and all other SPL related apps under COM-PLIANCE—SANCTION PARTY LISTS. The latest FIORI launchpad allows easy customization of the frequently used apps tagged to My Home and move around the apps as per the daily execution (see Figure 2.27).

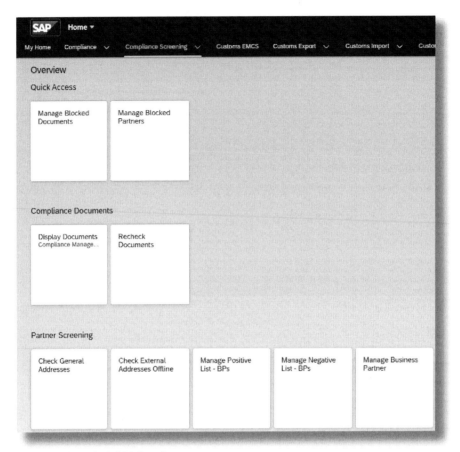

Figure 2.27: Fiori SPL landing screen

You can also view and navigate to all the Compliance related apps by clicking on the HOME dropdown button and scroll to COMPLIANCE—ADDRESS SCREENING and click on the desired app to directly open those Apps. See Figure 2.28.

If any of the Apps are missing, they can always be found on the App Finder under the user profile.

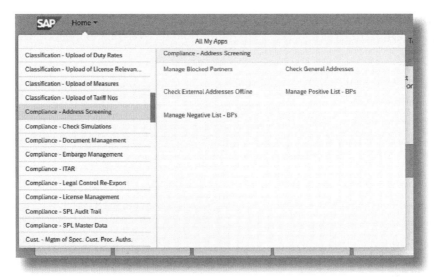

Figure 2.28: Navigating to required Apps

2.7.1 Business partner checking

Menu options

To view currently blocked partners, proceed to the MANAGE BLOCKED BUSINESS PARTNERS App see Figure 2.29.

The following options will be available to narrow your search. You can click GO without any refinements to see all blocked partners.

Figure 2.29: Display blocked business partner

Let's review some of the key fields available to filter the blocked partner list. Click on ADAPT FILTERS to see all the filter options available to select. See Figure 2.30.

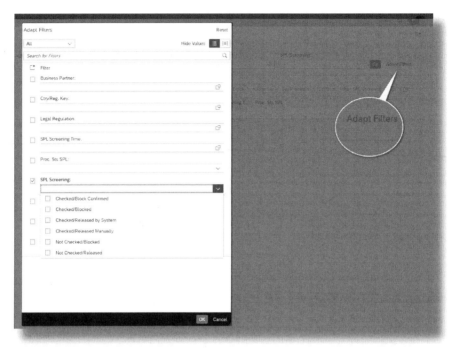

Figure 2.30: SPL Screening

To view only blocked partners, select the SPL SCREENING option as CHE-CKED/BLOCKED see Figure 2.30.

Figure 2.31: Country key

You can use this to display only blocked partners whose addresses are in the country or countries specified. For example, if you only wanted to see your North American blocks, you could list Canada, USA, and Mexico in the COUNTRY KEY field see Figure 2.31

Figure 2.32: BP number

You can use this to narrow your search to a specific partner or partners (see Figure 2.32). Note that this field refers to the GTS internal Business Partner number and NOT the external partner number (e. g., from your SAP ECC system). To refer to an external ID, see the field EXT. PARTNER NUMBER below.

If you have multiple Foreign Trade Organizations (FTOs), then you can use this to refine your search by specific FTO(s) (see Figure 2.33).

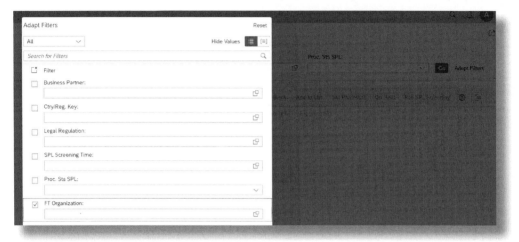

Figure 2.33: Foreign trade org unit

The following three fields can be ignored unless an EXTERNAL BUSINESS PARTNER is entered. If it is entered, then the other two fields will become required fields.

EXTERNAL BUSINESS PARTNER—refers to the number from your feeder system (e. g., customer number in SAP). You can paste a list of partners to see multiples.

LOGICAL SYSTEM GROUP—refers to your feeder system (e. g., SAP).

BUS. PARTNER CATEGORY—you can filter by partner type you want to narrow down. You can filter by Customer, Supplier, Person or Partner: Bank (see Figure 2.34).

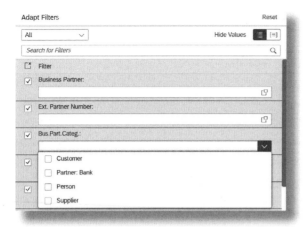

Figure 2.34: Business partner categories

Blocked partner view

As with most SAP search screens, you can save a specific set of criteria as a view. Once your choices are made, go to the dropdown menu beside STANDARD. After clicking on SAVE AS and providing a name for the view, click SAVE as shown in Figure 2.35.

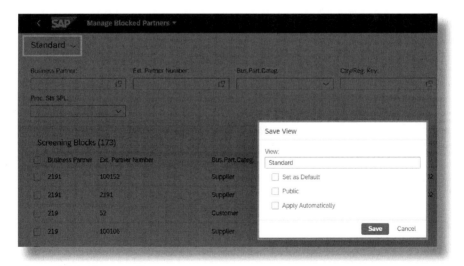

Figure 2.35: View attributes

The view will now be available on the main screen by clicking on the MY VIEWS dropdown list. The custom-made views can also be edited after selecting the view from the MY VIEWS LIST and clicking on MANAGE.

Reviewing BP blocks

After selecting GO, you will see all your currently blocked business partners (restricted by the options used in the menu, as described above) as in Figure 2.36.

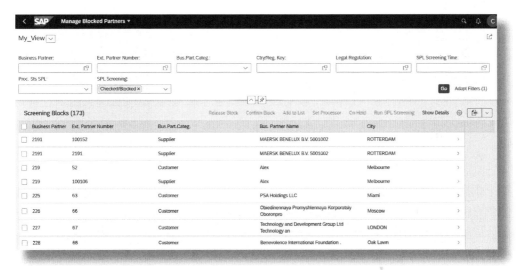

Figure 2.36: Blocked business partners

We recommend that you customize this layout to one that you find easy to use. You want to be able to see all the relevant data at a glance, without having to scroll to the right. A suggested layout is shown in Figure 2.36 (but you should design one that suits your own needs).

To change the layout, simply click on the SETTINGS button, which looks like a spreadsheet ⚙. Assign columns to be hidden or shown and rearrange the order as desired. Figure 2.37 displays suggested settings, but you can tailor the view however you wish.

Figure 2.37: Suggested layout

👉 **Save your layout changes:**

Remember to save your changes as a layout, or you will have to do this the next time you view the list.

To review the details of the block, simply click on the entry in question to review the block details.

Figure 2.38 shows a detailed analysis of a block called the *SPL Screening Details*. Let's take a closer look at the elements on this screen.

Figure 2.38: SPL Screening Details

SPL Screening Details

REFERENCE SECTION: This is your business partner from SAP ECC or other feeder system.

SPL HITS: These are the (one or more) SPL entities that have been deemed a "match" against your business partner, as per the configuration settings. You can see the SPL List they belong to and basic address information.

NAME MATCHES : These are the actual words that caused the match for you to review. In the new FIORI version, you will see that the actual matched words compared to the words in the business partner will be highlighted e.g., from Figure 2.38 GLASGOW **INTERNATIONAL TRADING**, **THE INTER-NATIONAL** BRIGADE is highlighted to match the words in the business partner "The International Trading Corp".

To view more details on the SPL entity, click on SPL NUMBER and the SPL entity master data screen will be displayed (see Figure 2.39). You can also see additional information such as expiration dates, complete names, and addresses.

In addition, the comments tab will often offer further insight into the SPL entry. You can check all the details provided by the data provider on the entity Birth Data, Identification, Comment, Government Agency and URL ref to the data provider website.

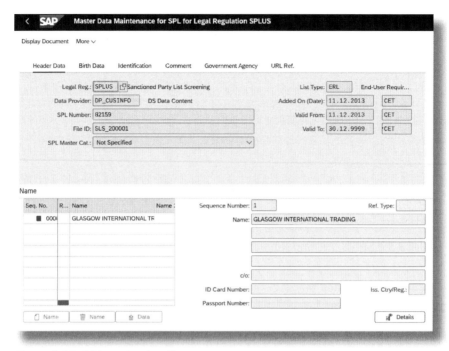

Figure 2.39: SPL entity details

Lastly, if your SPL data provider offers it, you may be able to launch its website from here for further information. An example from MK Data Services is shown in Figure 2.40.

Figure 2.40: URL reference tied to SPL entity

Based on the review above, you must now decide whether to release your business partner. Click BACK < to return to the results screen and make your decision. You cannot execute your decision in the audit trail screen.

COMMENT: If you need to leave some observations or notes concerning your analysis you can enter them in this section. If this is to be reviewed by another colleague, you can send information via comments (see Figure 2.41).

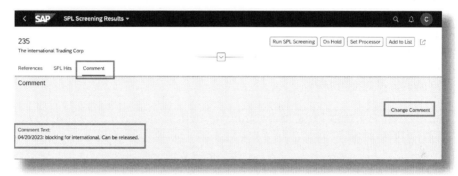

Figure 2.41: SPL Screening Comments

Releasing business partners

As explained, you must exit the detailed analysis/audit trail to affect a release decision. This is done primarily in the SPL SCREENING RESULTS screen. From this screen, you have the ability to perform several functions. In the sections that follow, we will provide a quick summary of the functions, as well as a more in-depth review of the release process (if you choose that function).

Functions

RELEASE BLOCK: Releases the business partner and allows it to be used in documents.

CONFIRM BLOCK: Confirms that the block is valid but will not place it on the negative list. Future users will be able to see this confirmation. It will not be usable in documents.

ADD TO LIST: Places the partner on the positive list or negative list. The positive list allows the partner to be used in documents. Positive list partners will not be checked with any changes in SPL entity. The negative list prevents the partner's use in documents.

SET PROCESSOR: Lets you either take responsibility for managing partners with the "Adopt" option, or to delegate partners to other users with the "Forward" option.

RUN SANCTIONED PARTY LIST SCREENING: Triggers a fresh screening of the partner against the current SPL lists. This is useful if you have reason to believe that the SPL lists have changed and a fresh screening will yield a different result (e. g., perhaps the SPL entity is expired now).

ON HOLD: Places the partner on hold, and future users will see that it is in a hold status. This is useful if you want to prevent another user from accidentally releasing the partner while you do further research. The partner will not be usable in documents.

As RELEASE PARTNER is the likely outcome in the majority of cases, we cover it in further detail below.

Release Partner

If you have made the decision to release the business partner, the typical process is as follows. From the SPL SCREENING RESULTS screen, click on the RELEASE BLOCK button as shown in Figure 2.42.

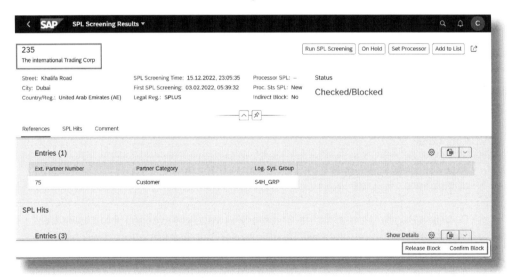

Figure 2.42: Blocked business partner release

Once you click on RELEASE PARTNER, you will see a pop-up screen for RELEASE BLOCK see Figure 2.43.

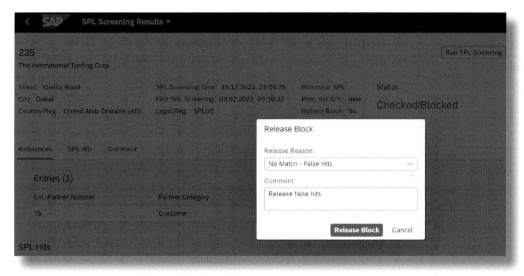

Figure 2.43: Release Block—Release reasons & Comment

On this screen, you can record the RELEASE REASON drop-down menu. This will bring up the various reasons you have assigned as options in configuration. There is no default or system-provided list of reasons; you must assign the reasons that make sense for your business.

☛ Reasons for release

We highly recommend that you set up reasons for release, as this is important for several compliance reasons, including:

▶ It forces the user to put some thought into why exactly they are releasing the entity.

▶ It provides an audit trail, and you can run reports showing why partners were released.

▶ It shows any future external auditor that thought (and due diligence) went into the release decision.

Secondly, you can enter text describing your reason for release. We recommend doing so when the release requires unusual research, or if you fear the release could be misinterpreted for any reason. If you enter text here, ensure that you save it by selecting RELEASE BLOCK. See Section 2.3.4 for a review of how to set up reasons for release and some suggested reasons.

Once you select RELEASE BLOCK, your partner is released, and the status of the block will be updated to Checked/Released Manually (see Figure 2.44).

Figure 2.44: Blocked Partner successfully released

You can mass block/release partners from the MANAGED BLOCKED PART-NERS view. You can select multiple partners which are already reviewed, and you can take any of the actions discussed above i. e., Release, Block, Add to List, Set Processor, On Hold or Run SPL screening (see Figure 2.45). Once you take a mass action to RELEASE BLOCK, the released partners will no longer show in the results screen.

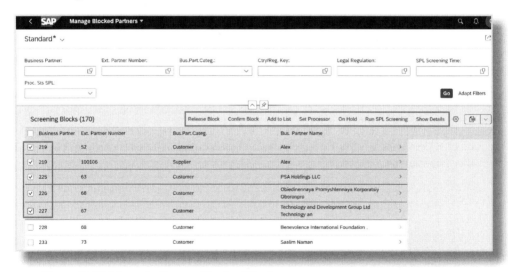

Figure 2.45: Mass Action on Blocked Partners

2.7.2   Document checking

Menu options

To view currently blocked documents, use FIORI app MANAGE BLOCKED DO-CUMENTS. If you want to give some users display only access, you can use FIORI app DISPLAY DOCUMENTS. Since most users want to release at the same time as they review, we are showing only the screen where you can do both. As discussed earlier, the new blocked document app shows all the document types. It is a one-stop location to manage all blocked documents.

Figure 2.46 shows the menu screen before you get to the results.

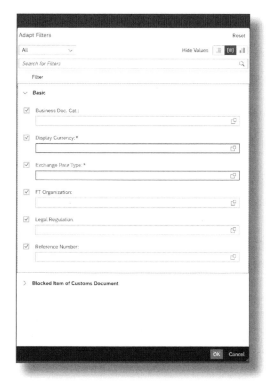

Figure 2.46: Release blocked document menu

The following options will be available to you to narrow your search. You can continue without any refinements to see all blocked partners. Some of the important filter parameters discussed below (see Figure 2.47).

Use FOREIGN TRADE ORG. UNIT to filter your results by FTO, such as a company division, country unit or the legal entity.

REFERENCE NUMBER isolates the document you are interested in if you know what it is. The REFERENCE NUMBER refers to the external document number (e.g., SAP ECC) and not the GTS document number.

Some of the other filter parameters includes blocking reason, Country of departure etc. (see Figure 2.47).

Figure 2.47: Document filter parameters

VIEW BLOCKED DOCUMENT

As with most SAP search screens, you can save a specific set of criteria as a view. Once your choices are made, go to the dropdown menu beside STANDARD. After clicking on SAVE AS and providing a name for the view, click SAVE, and you will be taken to the results screen (see Figure 2.48). The top half of the graphics called VISUAL GRAPHICS is interactive and you click the graphs to see the data details in the table view below.

In the next section, we will discuss the process for reviewing and then releasing the documents (if appropriate).

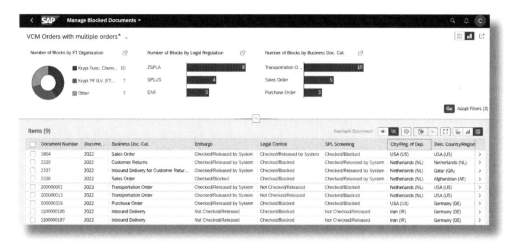

Figure 2.48: Release blocked documents results

Reviewing document blocks and releasing

Within the results screen, you can analyze the reason for the block by clicking on the DETAILED ANALYSIS button ⟩. This will show you an audit trail for the block, the same as it would in reviewing a blocked partner. However, unlike a BP review, the results can look different here, depending on the status of the partner used in the document.

This audit can have two results:

1. Show the SPL entry (or entries) that the document is blocked against (see Figure 2.49).

Figure 2.49: SPL block details for document with address check

2. Not show anything in the MATCHED SANCTIONED PARTY LIST ENTITIES SEC-
   TION (see Figure 2.50).

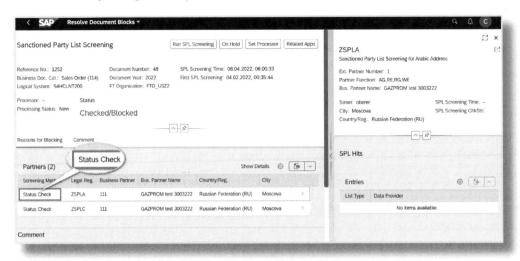

Figure 2.50: SPL block details with document status check

Each situation must be handled differently:

Situation 1—SPL entity shown in detailed analysis screen:

This typically occurs when the document itself has been checked using
the system's configured "match logic." For example, if the business partner used in an order or delivery was not blocked, but was the subsequently
edited in the delivery, it could cause a document block. In these cases, you
can see the results of the screening and review the audit details of the SPL
block.

When this occurs, you can release the document by using the RELEASE
BLOCK which will cancel the SPL block, or you can do a fresh SPL screening
using the RUN SPL SCREENING button to obtain the latest screening results
review and release document. When you decide to release the document,
you will see a pop-up for RELEASE REASON once you choose the reason the
document will be released (see Figure 2.51).

This report behaves the same way as it does in the business partner section.

Figure 2.51: Blocked document successful released

The RUN SPL SCREENING option is longer and takes you through a fresh screening of the partner. This is advised if the document has remained blocked for a length of time. It is a good idea to run the SPL screening again in case it now matches a new SPL entity (assuming you are doing regular updates to the SPL database).

Situation 2—No SPL entity shown in detailed analysis screen:

This occurs when the document is blocked as a result of a partner in that document already being blocked. You will not see the detailed audit trail for the block since the document was not truly audited—as soon as the partner was blocked, the document was also blocked. If you want to make sure future orders for the same partner have the correct screening results, you need to release the partner first. This is done through the regular MANAGE BLOCKED PARTNER app described in Section 2.7.1. Once the partner is released, you can use RECHECK DOCUMENT button, and the document will release. If you want to release just this document as an exception and decide not to release the partner, you can use the Release Block to release the document. Future documents with the same partner will block again.

> 👉 **It happens if the partner is blocked**
>
> Note that this will happen if the partner is blocked and not released yet, or if the partner is on the negative list see Section 2.7.3.

2.7.3 Positive and negative lists

Positive lists and negative lists remove the business partners listed from future checks. The *positive lists* ensure that the partner can always be used in documents without further blocks. The *negative lists* ensure that the partner stays blocked and will not be automatically rechecked. Until a user manually releases the partner from the negative list, all documents containing this partner will block. As will be clear, the positive list creates a large compliance risk and must only be used in the case of 100 percent guaranteed, safe entities that could not possibly be listed. We recommend great care and caution if you decide to use this function. Usually, if you have subsidies and intercompany entities that are giving rise to false hits on a regular basis, these are the best candidates to form part of the positive list.

There are four key functions related to the positive and negative lists:

1. Check positive list business partner address.

2. Check negative list business partner address.

3. Display positive list business partner.

4. Display negative list business partner.

Now let's walk through the two negative list functions in detail since you are more likely to use them than the positive list.

Please note that this area is intended for reviewing and rechecking listed entities. How an entity becomes listed is covered in Section 2.7.1—Reviewing BP blocks. If the user placed a BP on one of these two lists at the time of release, then this section is where you can review or recheck them to potentially remove them from the list.

Display negative list business partner

Use FIORI app MANAGE NEGATIVE LIST BPs see Figure 2.52 is used to view the partners that have been placed on the negative list. You can leave all of the options wide open, or you can narrow the search by multiple fields, such as country of the BP, date of SPL screening or BP number.

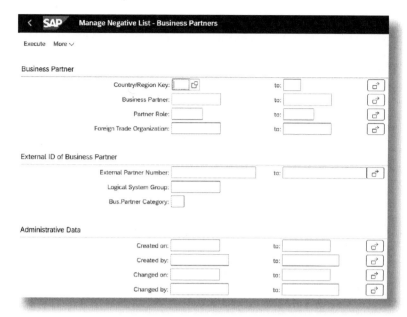

Figure 2.52: Display negative list menu

After you hit execute, you will be presented with the list of currently listed partners (see Figure 2.53).

Figure 2.53: Display negative list results

There is nothing more to be done on this screen. If you want to review the reason for a partners' listing, or take them off the negative list, you must go to the next function.

Check negative list business partner address

On this screen, you can re-screen a partner on the negative list. This will allow you to either leave it on the list or release it. This is typically done for two reasons:

1. A review of the listed party, either as part of a periodic review, or because you have reason to believe they should no longer be blocked.

2. A review of the decision to list a party, by a higher-level user. For example, a first-level review may have resulted in a negative listing, and that user's manager is now reviewing the decision as part of a second-level review. See Section 2.10 for a more detailed discussion of first- and second-level reviews.

When you run the Sanction Party List Screening from the screen shown above in Figure 2.53, you will be running rescreen and review of the latest screening results (see Figure 2.54).

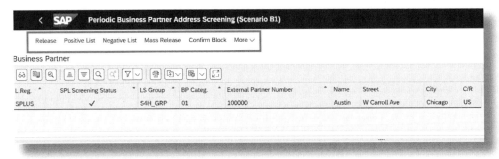

Figure 2.54: Rescreening results of negative list partners

This screen provides several choices. These choices are similar to those provided when you initially screen a business partner; however, there are fewer options since you are dealing with a partner on the negative list. Note that, after you make your decision and click the appropriate button, you will have to select SAVE to leave this screen.

▶ RELEASE: This will remove the partner from the negative list, and it is no longer blocked.

▶ POSITIVE LIST: This will move the partner from the negative list to the positive list.

▶ NEGATIVE LIST: This will return the partner to the negative list.

▶ MASS RELEASE: This will release all partners if you selected multiple partners on the menu screen.

To make sure the partners on the negative list are up to date, we recommend that the program check business partner on NEGATIVE LIST PERIODICALLY IN BACKGROUND is scheduled as a batch job based on a frequency that best suits your business to make sure these partners are reviewed.

We recommend that you specify a filter criterion on this screen (see Figure 2.55); otherwise, you will cause all listed partners to be rescreened.

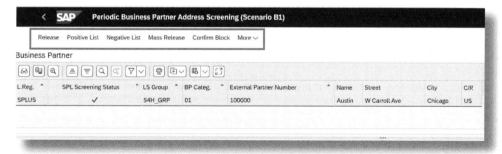

Figure 2.55: Periodic check for negative list menu

The same review process can be performed for business partners on the positive list. Use the FIORI app MANAGE POSITIVE LIST BPs to review positive list partners and you can review and act on the list.

2.7.4 Check external addresses

SAP GTS's most common use is in real-time communication with an ERP, typically SAP ECC or S/4. This is the ideal situation for compliance because it ensures real-time blocking and ongoing checking of partners and documents. However, the reality is that not all of the organization's operating entities will be on the same platform, and for at least a limited time, these parts of the company may not have real-time communication with SAP GTS.

In those cases, SAP GTS can still help using the CHECK EXTERNAL ADDRESSES (OFFLINE) functionality.

This part of the system allows for uploading an XML file, which will be checked against the SPL lists in SAP GTS. This is typically done with a customer list or a vendor list extracted from a system that is not linked to SAP GTS. These checks can be done as often as desired. Next, we will review how to run a check and go through the steps. For the purposes of the example, we will use a customer list.

The first step is to put the customer list into the required XML format. This is a template that is available to any SAP GTS user. The template is explained in SAP APPLICATION HELP, under XML STRUCTURE FOR ADDRESS

Data in Sanctioned Party List Screening. Once you have populated the data, you need to save it as an .xml file.

You only need to worry about the fields that you set up as significant in configuration. For example, if you do not compare telephone numbers in your SPL checks, then there is no need to populate this in the spreadsheet.

Next, go to the Check External Address (Offline) screen (see Figure 2.56).

Figure 2.56: Check external address screening

There are a few choices to consider before you click on execute:

1. Legal Regulation: Select the SPL legal regulation you normally use unless you have built one that is specially configured for offline screenings.

2. Group of External Log. Systems: You will need to create a new group for external screenings that differentiates it from the systems that are linked to SAP GTS.

3. PATH OF SOURCE FILE (LOCAL): This is a browse function similar to those used in Windows-based software. Use it to browse your local files (e. g., the "C" drive on your computer) and find the file containing the partners you want to screen.

4. PATH OF TARGET FILE (LOCAL): This is also a browse function, and you can use it to select the location of the results file (the file that shows the results of the screening, including which partners are "blocked" and which are not).

5. PATH OF SOURCE FILE (APPLICATION SERVER): This works the same as the local file version, except it means that you are looking for your file on a network server.

6. PATH OF TARGET FILE (APPLICATION SERVER): This works the same as the local file version, except it means that you are saving your results file on a network server.

7. XML FILE FORMAT: There are a few options available here; experiment with each one to determine your preferred layout.

8. Once you have made your selections, click EXECUTE to create a file in the target location you selected. This file will show which of the customers is considered a "blocked" match and which are not considered a "released" match. If you wish to review the screening results before you save you can check flag OUTPUT RESULTS.

2.7.5 Check General Address–Simulate screening

You may have scenarios where you might have a one-time partner that may not be set up as a partner and you want to review the partner or you get a request to review a partner. This option will be very useful to screen an address without setting them up in the system. This feature is also useful for evaluating the accuracy and completeness of the screening configuration, and for identifying any false positives or false negatives that may occur during the screening process. Use FIORI app CHECK GENERAL ADDRESS (see Figure 2.57).

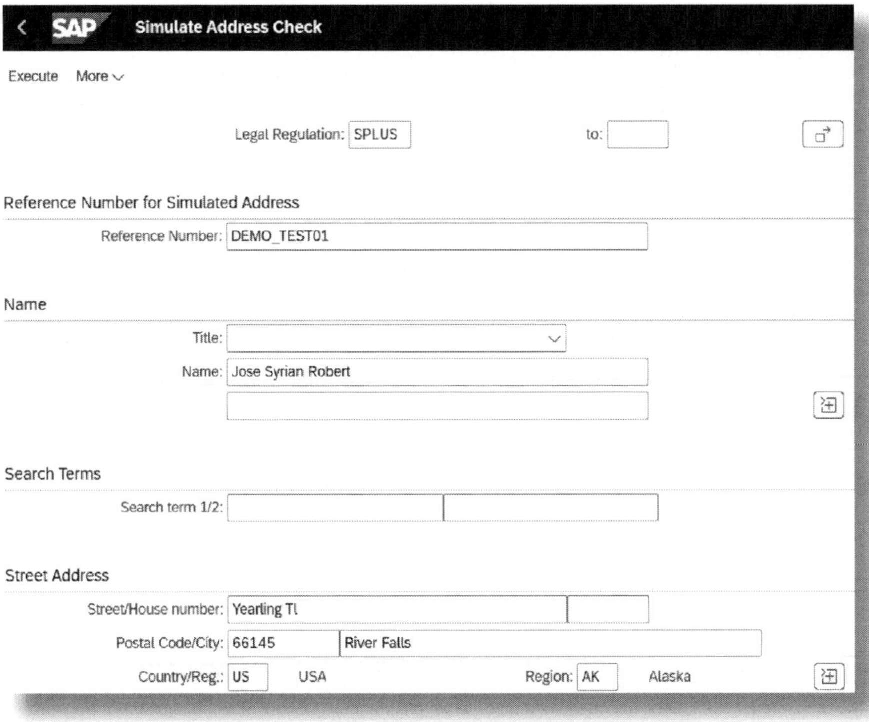

Figure 2.57: Check General Address—Simulate Address check

You can manually enter all the parts of a business partner's address. You can also give a reference number for the screening you are performing in order to review the results or audit at a later date. Once you enter the details you can execute to review the screening results as a regular partner screening. You will have an option to RELEASE or CONFIRM BLOCK and this will be saved as part of the audit trail.

2.7.6   Audit trail reporting

The audit trail section of SPL provides detailed and historical analysis of the SPL screenings that have been done in SAP GTS. It is a way to view screening results and user decisions. It is broken into four key categories: business partners, documents, external addresses and general addresses (see Figure 2.58). The results of the audit trail report look nearly identical for each.

Figure 2.58: FIORI Apps—SPL Audit Trail Reporting

Once you have the results of the audit trail report, we recommended building a customized layout (see Section 2.7.1 for a discussion on building a new layout).

The results of the audit trail can either be reviewed in SAP GTS or exported to Excel. The results will inform you of the result of the screening (block or not block), and in the case of blocks, will actually show you the SPL entity or entities that were matched, resulting in a block. Figure 2.59 shows a sample layout.

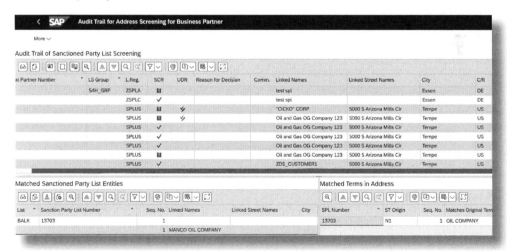

Figure 2.59: Audit trail for business partners

Audit trail for business partners

The menu for this function allows you to narrow your search using various options. Some of the key options include:

- ▶ COUNTRY KEY: Use this option to view the audit trail of all partners in a specific country. You may wish to do this periodically for high-risk countries.

- ▶ BP NUMBER: Use this option to narrow your search to a specific or multiple specific BPs.

- ▶ FOREIGN TRADE ORG. UNIT: If you have multiple organizations in play, this option allows you to review them separately.

- ▶ EXTERNAL PARTNER NUMBER: This option is the same as the BP number, except it uses your feeder system's number instead of the SAP GTS assigned number. Note that if you use this option you must also specify the LOGICAL SYSTEM GROUP and BP CATEGORY.

- ▶ CREATED/CHANGED/DATE OF CHECK: Use this string of fields to review specific date ranges.

- ▶ PROCESSING STATUS: This option is a great way to perform second-level reviews of partners that have been placed on hold or confirmed as blocked. See Section 2.7.1 for a detailed discussion of this process.

☛ Make sure you narrow your search

You must narrow your search in some way. Otherwise, the results will be so large that the system will either take an extremely long time to process or will outright fail!

☛ Purpose of "On Hold"

Many users wonder why they would use the "on hold" function instead of just leaving the partner blocked; here's why! It makes for a much cleaner audit trail and it also allows a level two user (see Section 2.10.4) to easily pull up all of the matches a level one user was unable to resolve.

Audit trail for documents

It is similar to AUDIT TRAIL FOR BUSINESS PARTNERS, and there are several options to narrow your search with documents. Some of the key options are:

- ▶ DATE OF SPL SCREENING: Use this option to narrow the search to a specific date range.

- ▶ OUTCOME OF SYSTEM CHECK: Use this option to only view screenings that resulted in a specific result. Typically, you would search only documents that were blocked by the system.

- ▶ OUTCOME OF USER CHECK: Use this option to only search documents that have had a user decision made for them, such as a release. This could be used to review all the documents that users have released, as an audit or second-level review.

- ▶ REFERENCE NUMBER: This means the external document number, e. g., an order number from SAP ECC.

Audit trail for external addresses

The options for this audit trail report are similar to the other two:

- ▶ DATE OF SPL SCREENING: Use this option to narrow the search to a specific date range. For example, if you uploaded an Excel spreadsheet, you would input the date you did that screening.

- ▶ OUTCOME OF SYSTEM CHECK: Use this option to only view screenings that resulted in a specific result. Note that even though GTS cannot truly block an external address, it will consider all SPL matches to be a "block" for this purpose.

- ▶ EXTERNAL PARTNER NUMBER: Refers to the address number that was contained in the XML file when it was loaded.

2.8 Master data

2.8.1 Maintain sanctioned party lists

Assuming you have gone with the recommended approach of using a subscription service for your SPL lists, this screen will really only be used for one purpose: to create and maintain a company-controlled SPL list.

The purpose of this list is to allow you to block partners that are not actually listed on any published SPL lists. Your company can have many reasons to use this function: a customer who failed to pay you, and you want to ensure they never get product again; a vendor engaged in unethical behavior, not serious enough to be listed as a government SPL, but serious enough for you to discontinue all business with them, or a true SPL entry from a list you chose not to subscribe to. As discussed in compliance tips, there are many SPL lists, and you may not subscribe to all of them. In that case, you may find some entities on those other lists you choose to block, and this is a way to get them into your system manually.

For obvious reasons, access to this function should be strictly limited.

2.8.2 Display Sanctioned Parties

Display sanctioned parties list is a way to review your populated SPL lists. This is a display only function, and as such, access to it can be shared with most users.

Users are able to call up all populated SPL entries and narrow the search using several options. The reasons why a user may wish to do so are varied, including to double check the accuracy of subscription data or as part of routine audits. Figure 2.60 shows the FIORI app DISPLAY SANCTIONED PARTY LIST. Some of the menu options are:

- ▶ TYPE OF LIST: Search only certain lists if desired, such as a particular Department of the Treasury Specially Designated National List.
- ▶ VALIDITY DATES: Narrow your search to only currently valid entries by limiting the validity date to the present and future.

▶ CHANGED/CREATED ON: If, for example, this was a subscription data audit, this option would allow you to view only those SPL entries that were created or updated in a certain date range so that you are not reviewing any that have been previously audited.

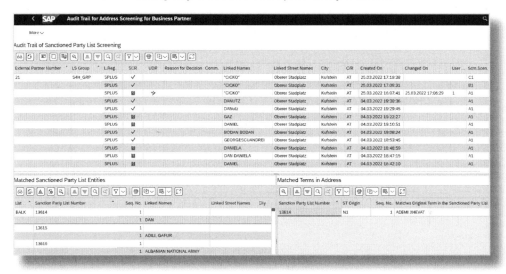

Figure 2.60: Display sanctioned party lists

2.9   Cross-area monitoring

2.9.1   Analyze reasons for release

This is a very useful report for auditing. You can use it to not only view the results of user decisions, as in an audit trail report, but also to capture the reason for release. This report is also a good way to review the users' work and ensure they are in fact using a reason for release. The FIORI APP ANALYZE REASON FOR RELEASE can be found under compliance Sanction Part List screening area shown in Figure 2.61; let's look at some of the key options on this screen.

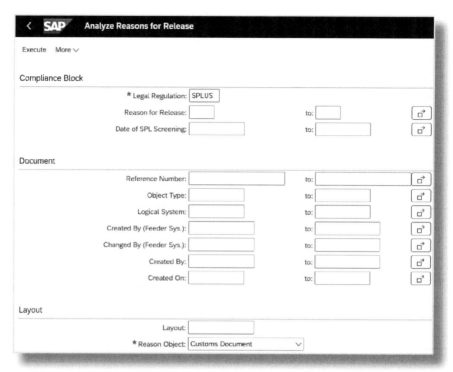

Figure 2.61: Analyze reason for release

▶ REASON FOR RELEASE: Use this option to only search releases done for a specific reason.

▶ DATE OF SPL SCREENING: This option narrows the search to the date of the SPL screening.

▶ REFERENCE NUMBER: This can refer to either a business partner number or a document number, depending on the choice you make in the REASON OBJECT field described below.

▶ REASON OBJECT: Use this field to specify either business partners or documents. Both options cannot be checked at the same time and must be audited separately.

2.10 Compliance tips

> **☞ Some common SPL misconceptions**
>
> Sanctioned Party List checking (also known as Excluded Parties, Restricted Parties, or Denied Parties) can be a confusing process to understand. It is a common misconception that there is a "list" to check against. It is also a common misconception that a law mandates checking against a list. The truth is, there are many lists, each of which comes from a different government or non-governmental source, and each list has unique implications and intentions. Furthermore, not everyone is equally bound by all lists, nor does each apply to all transactions equally. In this section, we will review the lists, including where they come from and why we check against them. We will also discuss best practices to follow when performing a check.

The following discussion is intended to assist you in developing your personal compliance plan. It is not possible to present a "canned" or ready-to-use plan, because every situation is different. Therefore, you must develop a customized plan for your business that takes into account all the risks you face and the unique needs and resources of your business.

2.10.1 Overview of SPL lists

In Appendix 2: Website resources, you will find a summary of various lists that are commonly checked against. As explained in Section 2.5.1, these list names and acronyms are taken from the data provided by Descartes (MK Denial). There are other sources of SPL data that may look different, but the information contained in the lists and the general structure of the lists should be largely similar.

These lists come from various sources but generally are created by a particular country's government agency or agencies (e. g., the US Department of the Treasury). Some lists, however, come from non-government agencies such as the United Nations Security Council or the World Bank.

Similar to the variety of sources for these lists, each list also has a different application that must be understood. For example, the Treasury *OFAC* lists tend to prohibit financial dealings of any kind with a listed party. On the other hand, the Bureau of Industry and Security's Entity List does not prohibit dealings but rather requires a license, and only for those items listed. In other words, you may be able to sell a truck to a listed Entity without a license but not a fighter jet. Furthermore, the BIS "Unverified List" does not prohibit dealings or require a license to do so. Instead, it is intended only to serve as a "red flag." There is no requirement to stop the transaction, but you are advised to do so and investigate further.

One thing to keep in mind is that, in most cases, there is no law requiring you to perform an SPL check at all. Rather, you are expected to comply with the rules of the list (e. g., not deal with prohibited parties), but how you achieve compliance is your own choice. Most government agencies will not tell you how to screen the list or how to deal with "close matches." Rather, they will simply penalize you if you break the rules.

Lastly, we would like to challenge the misconception that SPL checking is purely an "export" issue. True, exporting is a high-risk activity and far more likely to result in an SPL infraction than importing or domestic transactions. However, dealing with a forbidden party in any of the three transactions noted above can result in an offense as well. In fact, most Department of the Treasury offenses relate to financial transactions and dealings, **not** the movements of goods such as an export.

United States government lists

Lists created by the United States government get the most attention on a global level. This is for several reasons:

1. They are the largest.

2. They have the most serious enforcement and penalties.

3. Many companies operate in the US.

4. They apply "*extraterritorially*" (more on that later).

Because of the above, most compilations of SPL list data are dominated by those lists published by US government agencies. Figure 2.62 shows a web page offered by the US agency "export.gov" and is intended to assist

US exporters. It is important to understand, however, that some of the lists provided here apply to domestic transactions as well as exports.

Consolidated Screening List

Below is a link to a downloadable file that consolidates export screening lists of the Departments of Commerce, State and the Treasury into one spreadsheet as an aide to industry in conducting electronic screens of potential parties to regulated transactions. In the event that a company, entity or person on the list appears to match a party potentially involved in your export transaction, additional due diligence should be conducted before proceeding. There may be a strict export prohibition, requirement for seeking a license application, evaluation of the end-use or user to ensure it does not result in an activity prohibited by any U.S. export regulations, or other restriction.

Prior to taking any further actions, users are to consult the requirements of the specific list on which the company, entity or person is identified by reviewing the webpage of the agency responsible for such list. The links below will connect you to the specific webpage where additional information about how to use each specific list is contained. These links are also embedded into the file for each listed entity to direct you to the proper website for information about how to resolve the issue. Note that the column on the attached file, which is titled "Source List", indicates which specific consolidated screening list is the source for each entry on the spreadsheet. Blank data fields in the file are not applicable to the consolidated screening list in the "Source List" column.

Department of Commerce – Bureau of Industry and Security

- Denied Persons List - Individuals and entities that have been denied export privileges. Any dealings with a party on this list that would violate the terms of its denial order are prohibited.
- Unverified List - End-users who BIS has been unable to verify in prior transactions. The presence of a party on this list in a transaction is a "Red Flag" that should be resolved before proceeding with the transaction.
- Entity List - Parties whose presence in a transaction can trigger a license requirement supplemental to those elsewhere in the Export Administration Regulations (EAR). The list specifies the license requirements and policy that apply to each listed party.

Department of State – Bureau of International Security and Non-proliferation

- Nonproliferation Sanctions - Parties that have been sanctioned under various statutes. The linked webpage is updated as appropriate, but the Federal Register is the only official and complete listing of nonproliferation sanctions determinations.

Department of State – Directorate of Defense Trade Controls

- AECA Debarred List – Entities and individuals prohibited from participating directly or indirectly in the export of defense articles, including technical data and defense services. Pursuant to the Arms Export Control Act (AECA) and the International Traffic in Arms Regulations (ITAR), the AECA Debarred List includes persons convicted in court of violating or conspiring to violate the AECA and subject to "statutory debarment" or persons established to have violated the AECA in an administrative proceeding and subject to "administrative debarment."

Department of the Treasury – Office of Foreign Assets Control

- Specially Designated Nationals List – Parties who may be prohibited from export transactions based on OFAC's regulations. The EAR require a license for exports or reexports to any party in any entry on this list that contains any of the suffixes "SDGT", "SDT", "FTO", "IRAQ2" or "NPWMD"."
- Foreign Sanctions Evaders List: Foreign individuals and entities determined to have violated, attempted to violate, conspired to violate, or caused a violation of U.S. sanctions on Syria or Iran, as well as foreign persons who have facilitated deceptive transactions for or on behalf of persons subject to U.S. Sanctions. Transactions by U.S. persons or within the United States involving Foreign Sanctions Evaders (FSEs) are prohibited.
- Sectoral Sanctions Identifications (SSI) List: Individuals operating in sectors of the Russian economy with whom U.S. persons are prohibited from transacting in, providing financing for, or dealing in debt with a maturity of longer than 90 days.
- Palestinian Legislative Council (PLC) List: Individuals of the PLC who were elected on the party slate of Hamas, or any other Foreign Terrorist Organization (FTO), Specially Designed Terrorist (SDT), or Specially Designated Global Terrorist (SDGT).

Figure 2.62: Export.Gov consolidated screening list

> **❗ This is just a sample—there are many more lists to screen against!**
>
> Note, however, that this is not an exhaustive list of US published lists. In fact, if your data is similar to the data being used by most SPL screeners, over half probably belong to the GSA Excluded Party List.

GSA Excluded Party List

The GSA Excluded Party List is a narrowly focused list of entities debarred from GSA Government Procurement. The GSA is the General Services Administration, and they are responsible for the administration of the US Federal Government's real estate and infrastructure. They also manage certain aspects of government procurement, or selling to the government.

As a result of this function, they maintain a list of *excluded parties*. These parties are debarred from selling to the government because of some past infraction. The list of debarred parties is available at www.sam.gov, and most SPL list subscriptions include this data.

GSA Excluded Parties are usually only relevant if (a) you are selling to the government and (b) the item you sell to the government is somehow tied to an item or service you receive from the excluded party. That said, many companies deem it prudent to simply avoid dealing with GSA-excluded parties entirely.

Extraterritorial application of US lists

Something that is unique to the rules of the United States is that the US will enforce the application of these rules outside of the country. For example, many of the OFAC lists are stated as applicable to all "US Persons." In the regulations, a "US Person" is defined as (among other things) any US corporation and its subsidiaries. This means that a foreign subsidiary of a US company could be held liable for a business transaction involving a Department of the Treasury forbidden party, despite the transaction occurring in another country and involving neither US citizens nor goods originating in the US.

Because of this, it is well-advised that all companies screen against the US lists, regardless of whether or not they are operating in the US. There are many examples of the US applying its rules against foreign entities and individuals.

Other government lists

The US is not the only country that publishes lists of sanctioned parties. Canada, Australia, the United Kingdom, and European countries publish similar lists. While most of these lists are only binding for companies that operate or are owned in the applicable country, we recommend checking against all of these lists, for a couple of reasons.

Firstly, this will ensure you do not unknowingly violate a law. Many multinationals have very complex structures, and ownership of various divisions in different countries can often be surprisingly diverse. For example, you may be selling a good from Canada to Hong Kong, but the sales agent you employ for that region is an Australian citizen and lives there when not visiting customers in Asia. Do you know if the Australia Consolidated List may be binding on you? Better safe than sorry: it is better to review hits against foreign lists rather than to miss a violation when it is too late.

Secondly, different countries may spell foreign language names differently. For example, a name like Mohammed could be spelled as Mohamad by another country. Searching against multiple country lists will ensure the broadest range of spellings and varieties in your database, giving you greater security.

Non-governmental lists

There are also lists that are not published by the government, most notably, the UN Security Council and the World Bank lists. These lists are not binding in and of themselves, but parties on these lists are often added to local national lists as a result. Identifying a match before it becomes the law in your country is very wise. As a result, we encourage you to review these lists.

2.10.2 SPL List authorities and binding vs. non-binding

What follows is a non-exhaustive, quick reference guide to some common lists and advice on their binding nature and application, as well as the authority behind the list. This information should not be interpreted as legal advice; rather it is a suggested approach to SPL screening. As we indicated earlier, there is no law requiring SPL screening, only laws mandating that you do not violate the prohibition or obligations created by the list. As such, you are free to develop your own compliance method. The six examples provided below were specifically selected to show the wide variety of lists and their binding/non-binding natures. We encourage you to expand on this and do a similar review of all the lists to ensure that you have a complete understanding of the purpose and binding nature of the list in question.

GSA Excluded Parties List

Authority: General Services Administration

Binding for: Anyone selling to the US government, provided the sale to the government intersects with the activity involving the excluded party.

Application: Any purchase from the excluded party (goods or services).

Website: *www.sam.gov*

OFAC Specially Designated National Lists (e. g. SDNT, SDGT, SDNC)

Authority: Department of Treasury Office of Foreign Asset Control

Binding for: All "US Persons"

Application: These lists identify *SDNs* (Specially Designated Nationals). Depending on the specific SDN list, potentially any dealing in finance or goods and services is strictly prohibited (in other words, do not buy from them, and do not sell to them!).

Website: *http://www.treasury.gov/resource-center/sanctions/Pages/default.aspx*

> **! US OFAC lists are not only for companies in the USA!**
>
> Note that OFAC SDN lists tend to be extraterritorial. This means they do not only apply in the territory of the United States. Someone in a foreign country (e.g., Germany) could violate these rules if they are affiliated with a US company.

Example of OFAC *extraterritorial* reach: Let us look at the Global Terrorism list (SDGT) as an example: 31 CFR 594 prohibits dealing in property or money with a listed entity. The prohibition applies to all "US Persons." Section 594.315 makes it clear that a "US Person" includes the foreign branch of any US corporation. This is generally the case with all the OFAC sanctions.

BIS Entity List

Authority: Department of Commerce, Bureau of Industry and Security

Binding for: Anyone exporting or re-exporting US origin/content goods and US persons, regardless of the origin of the good.

Application: A license may be required for the export/re-export or in country transfer of any good to an entity on this list.

Website: *http://www.bis.doc.gov/*

World Bank List

Authority: The World Bank

Binding for: Anyone participating in a World Bank-financed contract.

Application: Any purchase from a listed debarred entity.

Website: *http://www.worldbank.org/*

United Nations Security Council Sanctions (UNS)

Authority: The United Nations Security Council

Binding for: Any UN member nation that has passed as law the resolution of the council.

Application: While a UN sanction is not immediately binding on any individual nation, it is virtually assured that most members will quickly pass it as law. Once it is passed as law (ratified), then it becomes binding in that country. We recommend considering any UN sanction as valid as law, as it will likely become law very quickly.

Website: *http://www.un.org/sc/committees/*

European Sanctions List (EUS)

Authority: European Union

Binding for: Any EU member state

Application: While the EU lists are technically only binding in the EU, many non-EU countries consider this the standard to follow. As a result, the EU lists are often copied by other countries, and we recommend that you monitor them, regardless of where you operate.

Website: *https://www.eeas.europa.eu/eeas/european-union-sanctions_en*

2.10.3 "Close matches" and what to do next

So, the software implementation is completed, the go-live date has come and gone, and all of the users are trained. The celebration party is already a distant memory. You are a user responsible for SPL releases and reviews. You come into work this morning and find a "match" resulting in a blocked document. You review the block and for the first time since you began using the software think you may be looking at a true match! The customer on your order may actually be the entity on the SPL list! Now what?

Unfortunately, too many users are put in this position and never properly trained on what to do with the software now that they have it. Certainly, they were trained on how to release the document. They were also shown how to place the customer on the negative list if it is a genuine match. However, they were never trained in the nuances of reviewing the SPL lists and how to deal with a "close match" or possible valid match.

Unfortunately, there is no easy answer to the question, "How do you verify a close match?" The Department of the Treasury does offer some guidance regarding how to determine matches. This information can be found on its website:

http://www.treasury.gov/resource-center/faqs/Sanctions/Pages/answer.aspx

However, you will very quickly note that this process instructs you to use it only if the "hit" is against an OFAC list. If it is another list, then it directs you to the "keeper" of that list. In practice, finding the "keeper" is not always easy. However, the guidance from OFAC is certainly good general guidance, and using these steps with any list is a good start.

☛ Department of the Treasury guidance

Step 1: Is the "hit" or "match" against OFAC's SDN list or targeted countries, or is it giving a "hit" for some other reason (e.g., "Control List" or "PEP," "CIA," "Non-Cooperative Countries and Territories," "Canadian Consolidated List (OSFI)," "World Bank Debarred Parties," or "government official of a designated country"), or do you not know what the "hit" is?

If the hit is against OFAC's SDN list or targeted countries, continue to Step 2 below.

If the hit arises for some other reason, you should contact the "keeper" of whichever other list the match is hitting against. For questions about:

The Denied Persons List and the Entities List, please contact the Bureau of Industry and Security at the US Department of Commerce at 202-482-4811.

The FBI's Most Wanted List or any other FBI-issued watch list, please contact the Federal Bureau of Investigation (*http://www.fbi.gov/contact*).

The Debarred Parties list, please contact the Office of Defense Trade Controls at the US Department of State, 202-663-2700.

The Bank Secrecy Act and the USA PATRIOT Act, please contact the Financial Crimes Enforcement Network (FinCEN), 1-800-949-2732. If you are unsure whom to contact, you should contact your interdict software provider that told you there was a "hit."

If you cannot tell what the "hit" is, you should contact your interdict software provider that told you there was a "hit."

Step 2: Now that you have established that the hit is against OFAC's SDN list or targeted countries, you must evaluate the quality of the hit. Compare the name of your account holder with the name on the SDN list. Is the name of your account holder an individual while the name on the SDN list is a vessel, organization, or company (or vice versa)?

If yes, you do not have a valid match.*

If no, please continue to Step 3 below.

Step 3: How much of the SDN's name is matching against the name of your account holder? Is just one of two or more names matching (e.g., just the last name)?

If yes, you do not have a valid match.*

If no, please continue to Step 4 below.

Step 4: Compare the complete SDN entry with all of the information you have on the matching name of your account holder An SDN entry will often have, for example, a full name, address, nationality, passport, tax ID or cedula number, place of birth, date of birth, former names, and aliases. Are you missing a lot of this information for the name of your account holder?

If yes, go back, get more information, and then compare your complete information against the SDN entry.

If no, please continue to Step 5 below.

Step 5: Are there a number of similarities or exact matches?

If yes, please call the hotline at 1-800-540-6322.

If no, you do not have a valid match.*

If you have reason to believe that processing this transfer or operating this account would violate any of the regulations, you must call the hotline and explain this knowledge or belief.

The instructions above outline how to determine a hit. The next question is, who should make that determination? We will explore this question in the next section.

2.10.4 Example of a review strategy

In the following section, we will review a sample process flow for an SPL review strategy. This process represents a two-level review, with an initial review by front line employees and the second performed by a manager or subject matter expert. The following is a quick summary of such a strategy, but keep in mind that every implementation must include a unique strategy that works best for the client. No two companies are alike in risk or structure, and no two strategies should be identical.

Note that this scenario assumes that the staff authorized to release are in distribution or logistics. In your case, they can be housed anywhere, but we strongly recommended that they do **not** work in an area with a vested interest in sales or purchases. For example, if the release staff were in the sales department, their decision to release could be compromised by their desire to make the sale. The ideal candidates are in compliance or legal if possible, but realistically, many companies will choose to place the function in logistics. Logistics departments typically are viewed as more of a neutral third party to transactions and willing to delay/stop them if they violate any rules or requirements. Also, note that this sample strategy is for business partner reviews. A separate review process for documents will also have to be created. The strategy is shown in Figure 2.63.

Step 1: The initial block

SAP GTS has identified a business partner (BP) that meets the criteria set up in your configuration settings. As a result, it is blocking the BP and it will remain blocked until there is a user review and release (if appropriate).

As soon as the block has occurred, an email alert is sent to the appropriate users. Only users with authority to release the block should receive this email, but it is recommended that both levels one and two receive it. Level two reviewers (for example, a department manager) may not respond initially, but this ensures they are aware of the block if their employees are unavailable, or refer it to them as a second-level review.

Step 2: First-level review

The first-level review involves front line employees, such as a Compliance Coordinator or a Logistics/Traffic Coordinator. These employees receive the email alert as soon as there is a block and go into the SAP GTS cockpit to review the reason for the block (as per section 2(a)(v)(1) in this chapter).

The release staff makes their decision based entirely on the data found within SAP GTS. There are three logical outcomes of their review:

1. They determine a "prima facie" false hit. This means the review determines that the hit is obviously, and on face value, not a real match. For example, if the SPL entry was John Wesley Smith, and the BP was Johann Smythe Wesley, under certain configuration settings, this may trigger a hit, but it is clearly a false hit. Using the steps OFAC suggests (as shown in Section 2.10.3) is a good way to spot false hits.

2. The match is valid (or possibly valid), but the SPL entry is expired. This will only occur if you have chosen to review expired entries in your settings (See Section 2.2).

3. The match is valid (or possibly valid), so it is referred to second-level review.

If the first-level reviewer encounters either scenario one or two, they are free to release the partner, and no further review is needed. If they encounter the third scenario (valid or possibly valid match), then it must be forwarded to second-level review. For the sake of this example, let's say that the second-level review is with the manager of the Logistics Department.

It should be easy to see that variations may be required across different companies and scenarios. A very simple example is that many companies may not be comfortable letting a first line reviewer release a match on account of an expired SPL entry and prefer this to be a reason for a second-level review.

Step 3: Second-level review

As we saw above, the first-level review is complete and the match is deemed valid, or at least the possibility of it being valid is sufficient to force a second-level review. The second-level review is likely triggered through an email or verbal conversation between the first-level second-level reviewer. Keeping with our example, our Logistics Coordinator sends an email to the Logistics Manager requesting a further review.

The second-level reviewer will perform a more detailed review that uses data outside of SAP GTS to further clarify the situation. In this model, there are three sources of outside data:

1. SPL Website. This means actually going to the source website for the government agency responsible for the SPL list in question. This is where more information is often found regarding the entry in question or it is possible to read the original executive order/federal register. You can also research the nature of the list and whether or not it means trade with that party is prohibited. You can read about this in Sections 2.10.1 and 2.10.2.

2. Other evidence or verification. This means plain old-fashioned investigation. Sometimes you will need to be a bit of a private investigator! If you enjoyed those old 1980s shows like Magnum PI, this will be right up your alley. Do some general internet searches to learn more about your

business partner. Will verifying some key point of data be important, such as birthdate or passport number? Consider going to a third party for assistance; there are now companies that offer consulting work that can range from researching your customer all the way to visiting them in person (anywhere in the world). Ninety-nine percent of the time, Internet research will prove adequate, but be prepared for when your sales manager will not allow the block unless you can prove this is, in fact, the SPL-listed entity.

3. Legal advice. If concerned, go to your internal or external legal resources for advice. You may be wondering why we never mentioned the option of asking the agency in question. This is because we would recommend leaving that task to legal, as they enjoy attorney-client privilege and can make a neutral inquiry. If you have reached the point where you are ready to say to an agency, "my customer may be on your list...," then leave that to the lawyers.

After all the research work, there are only two options: release the partner or leave it blocked. We recommend that, if you leave it blocked, that you place it on the negative list. This just makes for a cleaner audit trail and prevents accidental release by someone else.

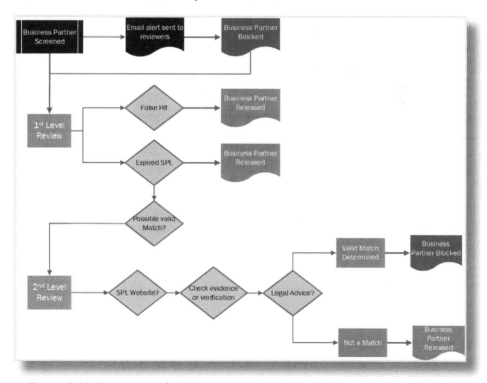

Figure 2.63: Recommended SPL review process

2.10.5 Auditing the system

You will want to implement routine audits of your SPL system. There are multiple components and aspects to the system, as discussed above, and due diligence requires you to audit its effectiveness. By "system," we do not simply mean "SAP GTS." We mean the comprehensive, total system around GTS, from configuration through to subscription services and end user training. Figure 2.64 shows a high level view of the SPL "chain," if you will. A weak link or break anywhere in this system could cause a failure and non-compliance. Every one of these sections must be audited periodically.

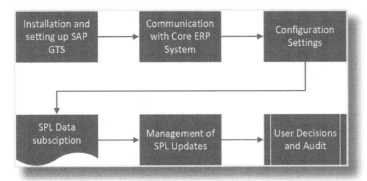

Figure 2.64: SPL chain

Suggested areas for audit:

The following section outlines some areas that we suggest you should audit. Please note that this list is not exhaustive.

GTS implementation

1. Was the implementation done correctly? Are all required settings in place?

2. Did the implementation ensure all types of partners and documents would be reviewed?

Communication with ERP

1. Are all documents transferring to GTS?

2. Are all new and changed partners transferring to GTS?

3. When do they transfer?

GTS configuration

1. Do the SPL checking settings ensure that all probable matches will be caught?

2. Would a real SPL entry be caught if used in a document?

3. What if that real SPL entry is spelt slightly differently?

SPL subscription data

1. Are all the legally required lists being checked?

2. Are the lists complete? (Do they match the government published lists?)

3. Are updates performed immediately? (e. g., if a new SPL party is listed by government today, when is it in subscription data?)

4. Are all SPL parties identified by their appropriate government list? (e. g., OF, AC SDN vs BIS Denied Party)

Management of SPL data updates

1. Are updates from the subscription provider sent as soon as they are created?

2. Are updates loaded into GTS immediately?

3. Are updates checked against previously released parties? When?

User decisions

1. Who is releasing documents/partners?

2. What training have they received?

3. Do they have a written release process to follow?

4. Who is checking their release history?

3 Compliance

Every business transaction that crosses a border, whether outbound or inbound, needs trade compliance checks. Compliance checks involve checking all the business partners that are in the shipping document against the sanctioned party list to make sure that the country being shipped to is not under embargo, as well as checking whether the product being shipped needs a license or license exception.

Say you have an outbound delivery. Before the delivery leaves, you must check the business partners to whom the item has been sold or shipped to, the bill-to party, the freight forwarder, and the third-party shipper. You also have to perform a sanctioned party screening against all business partners, check the countries associated with the ship-to party or the ultimate consignee where the product will land, perform an embargo check against the country where the product is being shipped, and determine the appropriate licenses against the ultimate consignee. So how does SAP GTS help?

SAP GTS can automate all of these checks to make the process faster and easier. You can configure the system to propose what licenses you will need and perform all your screening transactions and business partner checks against the denied party list. This only leaves the exceptions, such as potential matches on the denied party list, to be checked. Most importantly, your trade is not bottlenecked with manually performed compliance checks that can be unpredictable and error-prone.

3.1 Compliance checks overview

SAP GTS edition for HANA allows you to perform all necessary checks for both exports and imports, such as sanctioned party list screening, embargo screening, and license determination to import goods into the country. Furthermore, SAP GTS edition for HANA, allows you to support the monitoring of the transactions that are transferred to GTS, at various stages in the end-to-end sales and purchasing process. An overview of this close integration is shown in Figure 3.1.

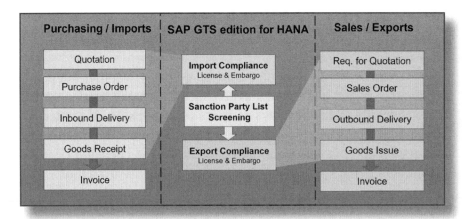

Figure 3.1: Import and Export Compliance integrated with Sales and Purchasing process.

SAP *purchasing process* involves various stages, including purchase requisition, purchase order, goods receipt, and invoice verification. By integrating SAP GTS, we can ensure compliance check as early as the moment a purchase requisition is raised. The checks at the purchase order level are continued to establish whether there are any import license required for importation. We can extend the Sanction Party List (SPL) screening for invoices to ensure banks are screened before the payments are processed.

SAP *sales process* typically starts with a customer request for a quotation. SAP GTS can be integrated at this level to make sure if any potential license needs to be applied which can also help in assessing the lead time for the order fulfillment. It is converted into a sales order, and then the delivery document is created once the order is ready to ship. At each level, SAP GTS integration helps ensure the order passes the compliance checks. Once the shipment is completed, the invoice is sent to the customer for payment. The inbound payment can also be activated for Sanction party list (SPL) screening to screen the payment banks.

All the orders passing through to SAP GTS for compliance check on the sales and purchasing side can easily be monitored under one Fiori App in SAP GTS edition for HANA. Monitoring allows you to review blocked documents (see Figure 3.2), follow the license assignment, and review assigned documents.

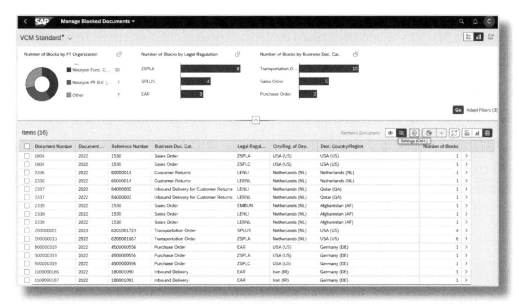

Figure 3.2: Manage blocked documents view

In this view you can see all different order type: Purchase Orders, Sales Order, Return Orders, Inbound and Outbound deliveries for all the blocked legal regulation in one place. This gives a comprehensive view for the trade compliance user to take various actions on the blocked document. Users can review and release the block, assign license and perform recheck of the document in this single Fiori app.

3.2 Legal control import/export

In the previous section, we covered import and export compliance from a business point of view, and in this section, we will cover how to address them in the system.

Legal control export/import allows you to enable the license determination for your outbound and inbound transactions (sales and purchasing). SAP GTS edition for HANA enhances the license determination functionality by allowing companies to meet complex license requirements. Many business rules and settings move to the SAP GTS Fiori launchpad for easy access and ongoing maintenance.

The expanded and enhanced functionality of SAP GTS compliance allows more flexibility to handle complex business processes. You can now enable different service checks, legal controls, embargoes, and sanctioned party lists (SPLs) by document type, item category, and item category-specific settings for inclusion of service checks. You also have specific legal controls for license types and certain control settings that enable you to meet complex license requirements. For example, you can enable value and quantity depreciations from transactions and multiple licenses attributes checks, such as products, export control numbers, business partners, and foreign trade organizations.

To activate these services with specific transaction types, the path is SPRO • SAP GLOBAL TRADE SERVICES, EDITION FOR SAP HANA • GENERAL SETTINGS • DOCUMENT STRUCTURE • ACTIVATE DOCUMENT TYPES FOR APPLICATION AREAS. Figure 3.3 shows the service activation for compliance with SAP GTS document types. You can selectively enable the services for document types.

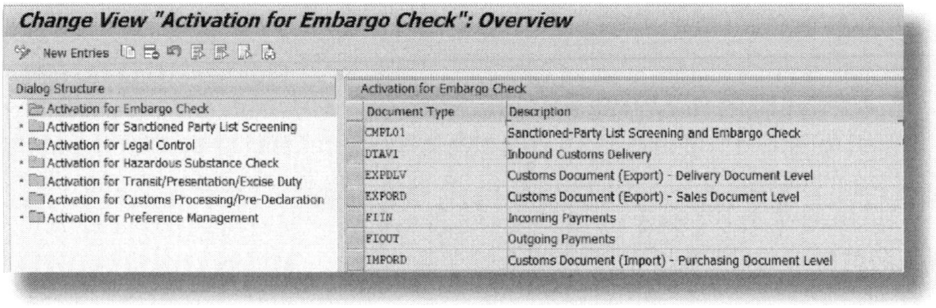

Figure 3.3: Document type activation for Embargo service

Activating SAP GTS Services against SAP GTS document types does not yet tell SAP GTS what to do with incoming SAP ECC documents. To link ECC documents with SAP GTS documents, follow menu path SPRO • SAP GLOBAL TRADE SERVICES, EDITION FOR SAP HANA • GENERAL SETTINGS • DOCUMENT STRUCTURE • ASSIGNMENT OF DOCUMENT TYPES FROM FEEDER SYSTEMS.

Figure 3.4 shows the assignment of the SAP ECC, S/4 HANA or your feeder system document types (sales, purchasing, and delivery) to an SAP GTS document. This allows you to set specific service checks for a particular SAP ERP or logistics document.

Change View "Mapping: Feeder System Group Doc. Typ

New Entries

Mapping: Feeder System Group Doc. Type to SAP GTS Doc. Type

Application Level	LS Group	Document...	Document Type
MMOA Receipt/Import: Purchasing Document ▼	S4H_GRP	EL	IMPORD
MMOA Receipt/Import: Purchasing Document ▼	S4H_GRP	FNB	IMPORD
MMOA Receipt/Import: Purchasing Document ▼	S4H_GRP	FZNB1	IMPORD
MMOA Receipt/Import: Purchasing Document ▼	S4H_GRP	FZNB3	IMPORD
MMOA Receipt/Import: Purchasing Document ▼	S4H_GRP	FZNB4	IMPORD
MMOA Receipt/Import: Purchasing Document ▼	S4H_GRP	FZUB1	IMPORD
MMOB Receipt/Import: Inbound Delivery ▼	S4H_GRP	EL	DTAVI
MMOC Arrival/Import: Goods Receipt Docum... ▼	S4H_GRP	101B	CULOIM
MMOC Arrival/Import: Goods Receipt Docum... ▼	S4H_GRP	101F	CULOIM
SDOA Dispatch/Export: Sales Document ▼	S4H_GRP	OR	EXPORD
SDOA Dispatch/Export: Sales Document ▼	S4H_GRP	TA	EXPORD
SDOA Dispatch/Export: Sales Document ▼	S4H_GRP	ZOR1	EXPORD
SDOA Dispatch/Export: Sales Document ▼	S4H_GRP	ZOR2	EXPORD
SDOA Dispatch/Export: Sales Document ▼	S4H_GRP	ZOR3	EXPORD
SDOB Dispatch/Export: Outbound Delivery ▼	S4H_GRP	LF	EXPDLV
SDOB Dispatch/Export: Outbound Delivery ▼	S4H_GRP	LO	EXPDLV
SDOB Dispatch/Export: Outbound Delivery ▼	S4H_GRP	ZLF3	EXPDLV

Figure 3.4: Mapping feeder system document types to SAP GTS

In SAP GTS, you can define document types by the services you want to activate. For example, the service order involves service-related contract and billing, excludes no material shipment from the part number of the license determination check, and performs only SPL and embargo checks. This way you have more flexibility in terms of what services you want to invoke, selectively by order types and within the item category level. You may have licenses that are value- and quantity-dependent. SAP GTS allows you to define a depreciation group for value and quantity. When you have a license created for a specific quantity and value based on the transaction value and quantity, the license consumes and depreciates them. Figure 3.5 shows the VALUE and QUANTITY DEPRECIATION set up BY ITEM CATEGORY and DEPRECIATION GROUP.

Change View "Item Categories / Legal Regulations": Overview

New Entries

Dialog Structure
- ☐ Activation for Embargo Check
- ☐ Activation for Sanctioned Party List Screening
- ☐ Activation for Legal Control
  - ☐ Item Categories / Legal Regulations
- ☐ Activation for Hazardous Substance Check
- ☐ Activation for Preference Processing
- ☐ Activation for Letter of Credit Processing
- ☐ Activation for Restitution

Item Category EXDLY1

Item Categories / Legal Regulations

Leg Reg	Description	Qty Depreciation	Value Depreciation	Consider Validity	
LMI	Export Administration Regulations	Depreciation: Deduct... ▼	Depreciation: Deduct... ▼	Include Both "Valid From" a... ▼	
NAFTA	North American Free Trade Agreemen...	Depreciation: Deduct... ▼	Depreciation: Deduct... ▼	Include Both "Valid From" a... ▼	

Figure 3.5: Item category activation

3.3 Embargo checking in SAP GTS

Today's world of trade requires your business to be able to ship and receive goods as quickly as possible. You must be ready at a moment's notice. At the same time, governments also work just as quickly. Relationships between countries change quickly and you must be ready for this as well. The best way to be prepared for global changes is using embargo checking. *Embargo checking* allows you to screen the ship-to country for export partners and ship-from country for import partners. It also allows you to block any transactions shipped to or from embargo countries.

Embargo checking is performed when a business partner is created. Therefore, if you have a business partner created in ECC and transferred to SAP GTS edition for HANA, it will screen the business partner for an embargo. With business partner transfer, if screens the business partner against the embargo list maintained in GTS. If it finds a match, it blocks the customer for embargo.

With regards to transactions, you might use a sales order or stock transport order, followed by an outbound delivery note, to ship out the product. When a sales order is created, the Business Partner (BP) will be reviewed against the BP embargo checking, and if the customer is blocked for embargo reasons, it will block the sales or any outbound transaction. The GTS block on the sales document allows you to configure it to stop the further processing of the sales document; that is, stop the delivery note creation. Similarly, in the case of a purchase order, if you have a vendor under embargo block, the system checks for the embargo block with the vendor and blocks the purchase order.

SAP GTS edition for HANA manages embargo situations as services within compliance, and you can control the different legs for embargo or maintain different country list regulations. Most importantly, the SAP GTS edition for HANA master data maintains these countries, which means you do not have to go through configuration settings. Figure 3.6 shows the embargo setting with the SAP GTS edition for HANA. You can access app MANAGE EMBARGO SITUATION under group EMBARGO CHECKS.

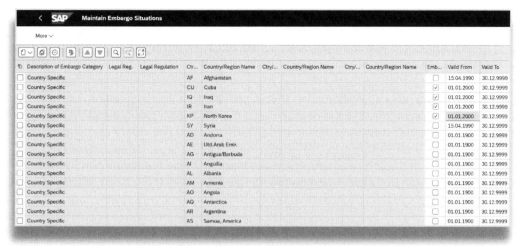

Figure 3.6: Embargo settings in SAP GTS master data

Using the country-specific information allows you to list all of the countries that you ship to or ship from. You can check the EMBARGO box to activate embargo for a time period.

Many embargos apply to both imports and exports. For embargos limited to a specific direction (inbound or outbound), you can use the same app MANAGE EMBARGO SITUATION but choose the option legal regulation country of departure designation.

Description of Embargo Category	Legal Reg.	Legal Regulation	Ctr...	Country/Region Name	Ctry/...	Country/Region Name	Ctry/...	Country/Region Name	Emb...	Valid From	Valid To
Legal Reg. C/R of Departure/Destination	EMBUN	Embargo - United Nations	UA	Ukraine					✓	01.01.1900	30.12.9999
Legal Reg. C/R of Departure/Destination	EMBUN	Embargo - United Nations	SY	Syria					✓	01.01.1900	30.12.9999
Legal Regulation/C/R of Departure or Des	EMBUN	Embargo - United Nations			US	USA	RU	Russian Fed.	✓	01.01.2022	31.12.2025

Figure 3.7: Embargo setting based on country of departure/destination

Figure 3.7 shows the master data maintenance for embargo based on the country of departure and country of destination. In the legal regulation, you create an entry for LEGAL REGULATION/C/R OF DEPARTURE OR DES and select in the LEGAL REGULATION first country field the country of departure and in the second country field the country of destination. Choose a validity period for this embargo situation. Legal regulation represents the highest entity in GTS against which the different GTS services are configured and data services are activated.

You can also have an embargo list that is specific to a legal regulation. Legal regulations represent the country legal customs laws and regulations. In the example shown, the regulation is EMBUN, but you can create as many regulations as necessary. In this screen, maintain the legal regulation and the country of departure or country of destination. Legal regulation can be active for export or import, and based on the activation, the country listed here will apply to those transactions (export/outbound or import/inbound).

3.4   Product classification

All goods shipped out of the US must be labeled with their five-character *Export Control Classification Number* (ECCN), license or license exception, and *Schedule B* or *Harmonized Tariff Number*. ECCN are associated with the product and describe its classification, which category or group and relevant control it falls under, or lack of it applies. Without a Schedule B, you cannot complete the Shipper's Export Declaration (SED), and other export declaration documentation requires these three critical pieces of trade information: ECCN, Schedule B, and License or License exception, if applicable. Furthermore, you also need a Harmonized Tariff System number for import into any country around the world. You need to be able to access these numbers quickly and easily. The classification tool in the SAP GTS edition for SAP HANA facilitates searching for the right number and allows you to classify and assign the classification number to a product. As product classification is a daily and ongoing activity for trade, you can pull up a work list at any given time to see products that require classification. The classification work list is one of the tools available with SAP GTS Edition for SAP HANA that allows you to prepare for your day-to-day work and plan your workload.

In SAP GTS edition for SAP HANA, only the classification definition is done within the configuration, and the actual control of data is maintained within the front end as master data. In SAP GTS edition for SAP HANA, classifications are controlled by a numbering scheme, and you can even configure the structure to represent the number. In Section 3.8 we have also described how to define your own numbering scheme with a customized structure.

☛ **Export Control Classification Number**

An *Export Control Classification* **Number** (ECCN) is a specific alphanumeric number used to identify the level of control for an article being exported from any of the 40 countries participating in the Wassenaar Agreement. In the US, the ECCN is assigned by the Department of Commerce.

The *Harmonized Tariff System* is an internationally standardized system maintained by the World Customs Organization (WCO) for classifying traded products. Usually made up of six to ten digits, the Harmonized Tariff System classifies products for customs purposes.

3.4.1 Classification data maintenance

In SAP GTS edition for SAP HANA, product is classified by legal regulations. Legal regulations are defined for a country, and every regulation has an originating country. Classifications can also be set up for country groups if they are shared across multiple countries. If you have more than one country where the same regulation applies, you can activate this regulation to apply to all applicable countries. In other words, you can maintain the product classification per regulation activated only by countries where this regulation applies.

You can use the ECCN to represent the export control with the product classification and the ECCN grouping to further sub-classify and add another layer of control for the license determination or control. For example, if you have an ECCN that has a different control for retail and non-retail, you can use the ECCN group to represent retail and non-retail. Therefore, you have an ECCN that translates to the ECCN control as published by the customs authorities, and the ECCN grouping could then be used for granular control, with the same ECCN used for retail and non-retail. An ECCN group can be maintained using the FIORI App MANAGE CONTROL GROUP FOR PRODUCTS found under COMPLIANCE—LEGAL CONTROL CLASSIFICATION.

As compared to earlier versions of SAP GTS, the numbering scheme configuration has been simplified in SAP GTS edition for HANA.

SAP GTS edition for HANA also allows you to upload an XML file through the classification content, or you can maintain it manually in the system.

The classification content or classification codes for import and export are identified and maintained as a numbering scheme. SAP GTS edition for HANA allows maintenance by following groups of numbering scheme which serve for different scenarios and purposes:

▶ Tariff Numbers—for Import

▶ Commodity Codes—for export

▶ Control Classes—for license and legal control

▶ FDA Product Codes—specialty codes for additional government agencies

▶ Excise Duty Codes—specific type of duties or tax codes

All the above numbering scheme configurations involve following three steps. These steps are explained in reference to tariff number but the same steps apply to other types as well.

▶ Define Numbering Scheme –choose the length, reference scheme (if any), measure scheme and flag to exclude redistribution to feeder systems (see Figure 3.8).

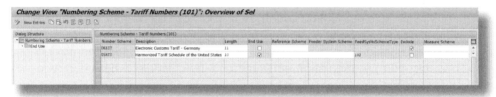

Figure 3.8: Defining Numbering scheme

▶ Define Numbering Scheme Content—Define the content source (manual or external data provider), structure of the content, additional procedures and restrictions (see Figure 3.9).

▶ Activate Numbering Scheme Content—in this step we build the relationship between the numbering scheme and scheme content. Many numbering schemes can share the same scheme content (see Figure 3.10).

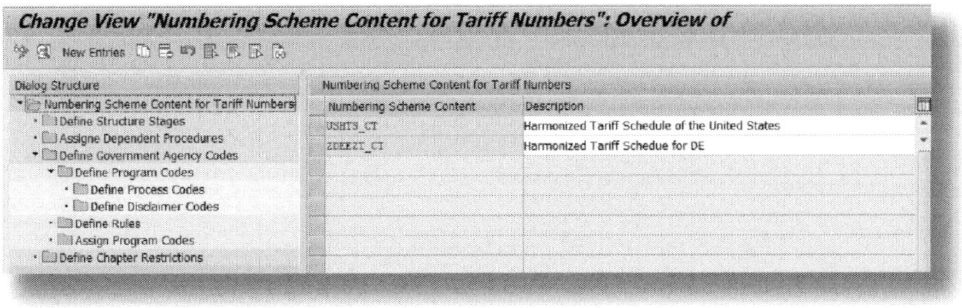

Figure 3.9: Numbering scheme content

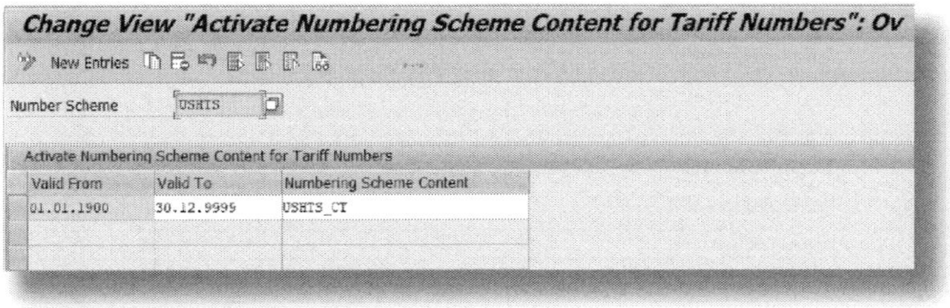

Figure 3.10: Activate numbering scheme

Based on the structure maintained in the configuration, the content can be loaded or manually maintained within SAP GTS edition for HANA. A detailed step by step example on defining and maintaining numbering schemes and content is explained in Section 3.8

SAP GTS edition for HANA allows you to classify or assign an import or export classification to a product using three different Fiori apps:

1. Classify Product

2. Manage Products

3. Reclassify Products

These three different classification tools facilitate product classification. Classify products provides a list of products that require classification.

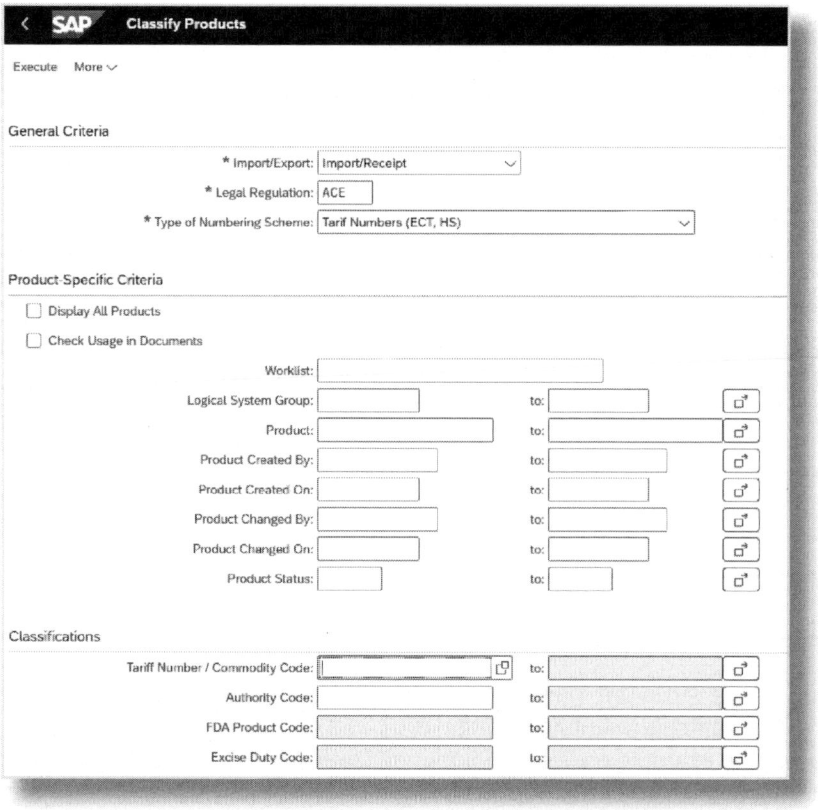

Figure 3.11: Classify Product

Classify Products is a Fiori app as shown in the selection screen in Figure 3.11. You can filter based on the data selection available. Based on the data selection, users can work on the list of products. The output list also provides functionality to mass assign the classification to products. In other words, if you have multiple products falling under the same classification, you can use the mass assignment functionality to assign the same classification to all the products, instead of assigning one at a time. This app also has two filter options available on the selection screen to effectively use the worklist. *Display all products* shows products that are already classified. It is very helpful in finding how similar products are classified and can be copied or changed. The same option allows you to extract a query for all classified products. *Check Usage in Documents* is a flag with which you can filter only those products that are matching the selection criteria and also appears on a transactional document like Sales Order or Purchase Order in SAP GTS.

To access this app, go to SAP FIORI LAUNCHPAD, search for CLASSIFY PRO-
DUCTS app or find the Classify product app under the CUSTOMS—CLASSIFI-
CATION group Manage product functionality allows you to classify multiple
classification like ECCN, harmonized tariff system and tax classification in
one view.

Figure 3.12 displays the function providing different tabs for classification.
Within the LEGAL CONTROL tab, it is possible to classify the ECCNs for different regulations. In the CLASSIFICATION tab, you can assign the HARMONIZED
TARIFF SYSTEM and in TAX CLASSIFICATION tab you can assign tax code for
various countries.

Figure 3.12 shows the export and import classification assignment to a
product. On this screen, you can see all the regulations that are actively
listed and the numbering scheme for the regulation where the harmonized
tariff and commodity code number is assigned. You can go to this app from
the SAP FIORI LAUNCHPAD search for MANAGE PRODUCTS app or find the MA-
NAGE PRODUCT app under PRODUCTS group.

Figure 3.12: Classify product screen

Reclassification allows you to change or assign a new classification number to the product. In other words, if you have a classified product, you can
use reclassification to change it to a new number. Customs authorities
periodically publish changes to the classification, which might affect your
product classification, and you can use this function to apply the changed
classification to the product. When you click on the reclassification transaction, the report will propose the old classification number and a new classification number. When you execute, it replaces the existing number with the
new number you entered. Like other features for export, import, commodity

code, and harmonized tariff number, SAP GTS edition for HANA provides functionality to reclassify the respective numbers manually or through an XML upload file. You can find the RECLASSIFY PRODUCTS MANUALLY app under CUSTOMS—CLASSIFICATION group or you can search for the app RECLASSIFY PRODUCT or RECLASSIFY PRODUCTS XML-BASED upload file. Figure 3.13 shows how to mass reclassify all the products due to a change in classification from an existing code 0401100000 to a new code 0401205000. Once the system validates the old and new code it automatically lists all the products and you will have the chance to override any products that are not supposed to change.

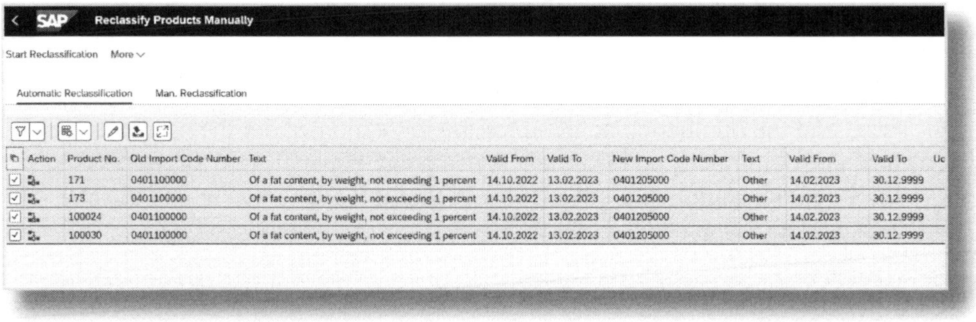

Figure 3.13: Reclassify products

3.5 Classifying variant configurable products

SAP Variant Configurable Product is a type of product that can be customized or configured by the customer using predefined or selectable options. This allows customers to order a product that meets their specific requirements or preferences. From a master data point of view, there is no need to maintain multiple discreet materials of each of those combinations. Due to the nature of variant configurable products, HS tariff classification for some of these products might change depending on the characteristics like length, width, size and color. This becomes a challenge to have the classification maintained for such products in SAP GTS. In this section you will find a standard way of maintaining multiple tariff codes for a product and how we could automatically choose the right tariff at the order level.

Let's say we have a product that is a type of tape or sheet. The tapes can be classified under different HS codes depending on its length or width. If the tape is less than 20 centimeters wide, it would be classified under HS code 3919.10, which is the HS code for tapes in rolls of a width not exceeding

20 cm. If the tape is 20 centimeters or wider, it would be classified under a different HS 3919.90.50.

End Use activation—Activate numbering scheme to allow multiple classifications for a product by using the End Use functionality in GTS. End use definition is based on different characteristics the HS codes of which vary. You could define them by characteristics or you can group them or create levels of HS codes. In our above example of tapes by length it is considered as levels. To define new END USE follow the customizing path SPRO · SAP GLOBAL TRADE SERVICES, EDITION FOR SAP HANA · GENERAL SETTINGS · NUMBERING SCHEMES · TARIFF NUMBERS · DEFINE END USES as shown Figure 3.14.

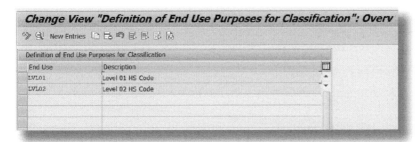

Figure 3.14: Define different End Use to store multiple HS codes.

Assign End Use to HS tariff scheme—The End Use created above should be assigned to the HS tariff schema Follow the customizing path SPRO · SAP GLOBAL TRADE SERVICES, EDITION FOR SAP HANA · GENERAL SETTINGS · NUMBERING SCHEMES · DEFINE NUMBERING SCHEME FOR TARIFF NUMBERS as shown in Figure 3.15

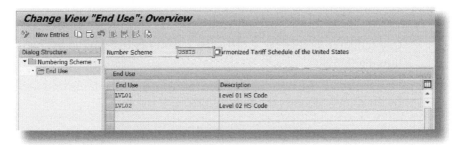

Figure 3.15: Assign End Use to Numbering scheme

Classifying products with multiple HS codes—Once we have activated END USE, we can save multiple HS codes for the same product at master data level using the CHANGE PRODUCT app. Figure 3.16 below shows assigning two codes 3919.90.50.60 as level 1—LVL01 END USE code and 3919.10.10.50 as level 2—LVL02 END USE code.

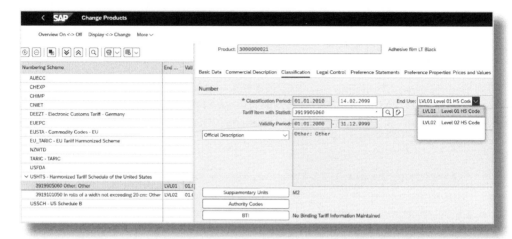

Figure 3.16: Product classification with multiple HS code assigned.

Order level HS determination—Enhancement to automatically select the right HS code at order level. Now that we have assigned two HS codes for the product, we can pick the right HS code at order level based on the length characteristic with an enhancement during the order transfer from SAP ECC or S/4 system to GTS.

Implement the user exit for transfer of MM and SD Documents (Enhancement Project SLLLEG01) and the function exit EXIT_SAPLSLL_LEG_CDPIR3_002. Following logic explains how to determine variant configuration characteristics and send the right end use for GTS to determine the correct HS code.

▶ Use function module VC_I_GET_CONFIGURATION to read the VC configuration table.

▶ Find the width characteristics from the configuration table returned by the above function module.

▶ Apply the logic to compare the width of each variant config line item on the order, if width is greater than 20 CMS `cs_api6800-item-gen-product_enduse` = "LVL01" else, `cs_api6800-item-gen-product_enduse` = "LVL02" this end use should match with the HS code assigned in GTS (see Figure 3.16).

▶ We can also determine the product end use as a characteristic by writing this logic in variant configuration script and pass the end use to GTS.

▶ Any variant configuration characteristics can be used to apply the same logic i.e., size, color, material etc., to determine the HS code.

3.6 License determination

License determination is among of the most important functionality in any global trade compliance solution. In any business transaction, be it purchase orders or sales orders, you are dealing with business partners (vendors, customers) and a product or service. The product or materials being shipped are given a number and description that is understood by your customer and vendor. For exports or imports, products are classified further so that the customs authorities understand them in the exporting and importing country.

Usually, the exporting country imposes control over products based on the classifications. For example, certain products based on the classification might not be allowed for export to a certain country or customer due to its application and risk. Some products may be allowed, but only with the permission of the controlling agency in the form of a license.

Some products might generally be subject to a license requirement but be eligible for certain license exceptions. This means that they generally require an export license, but in certain circumstances, do not.

As you can see, the license landscape is complex, requiring an understanding of classifications, license requirements, and exception possibilities.

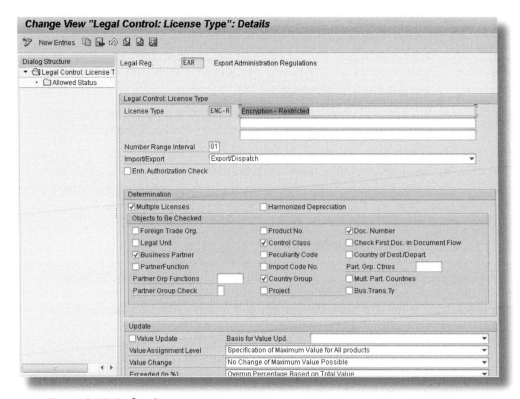

Figure 3.17: Define license type

SAP GTS edition for HANA has enhanced this license type by adding more attributes and features (status, control settings, partner type checking, and customer-defined procedures for license type determination). More attributes allow you to define licenses with stricter control and accuracy. For example, before a license can be assigned, all of these attributes must be satisfied. Use the ALLOWED STATUS functionality to maintain the status for a license, such as active or expired. Figure 3.17 shows the definitions available in the license types in SAP GTS edition for HANA.

As you can see in Figure 3.18, there is functionality to check multiple agreements, which allows you to check multiple licenses to fulfill a quantity or a license requirement. For example, if your particular license does not meet the quantity requirement, the system can look for another license value to meet the remaining quantity. You can also define the percent overflow for tolerance. For every attribute selected, you can select how many values you want maintained in the system.

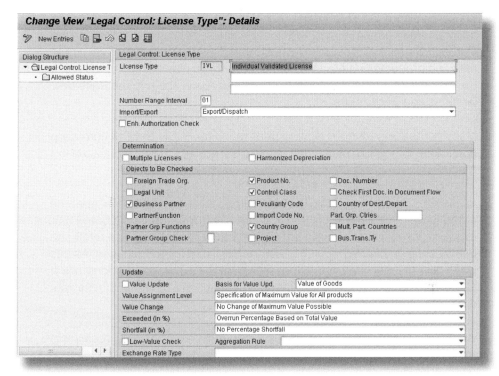

Figure 3.18: Configure license type

Export or import regulations require a determination process to see if a license is required. The license determinations consider the product classification, and based on the classification, determine if a license is necessary. The results can be:

▶ License required

▶ No license required

▶ License required but exception available

Classifications are assigned to products and based on the country of departure or destination; the system picks up the relevant legal regulation and uses the license determination table to determine the license types. License types are codes that represent licenses, exceptions, or no license required in the system.

SAP GTS edition for HANA moves trade data to business user access within the master data, one of the frequently maintained and updated information. In addition, SAP GTS edition for HANA provides programs to upload the content through XML interfaces. With SAP GTS edition for HANA, you maintain trade data manually with tools available to maintain them. Use the Fiori app MANAGE CONTROL CLASSES to maintain the classifications. Trade data and products need to be assigned with these classifications to enable the export and import compliance check and report them in the trade declarations and documents.

Many companies take the approach of mapping ECCN to ECCN grouping one-to-one in order to enable the LEGAL CONTROL • LICENSE DETERMINATION function.

In SAP GTS edition for HANA, the ECCN group can be an additional attribute to the product classification, and you can use it for additional control. For example, if you want to have a different control for retail and non-retail, you could define an ECCN grouping to control the license determination. As this is the core of legal control, and they represent the export control for product shipment, the SAP GTS edition for HANA launchpad maintains these with the trade user access.

COUNTRY GROUP consists of multiple countries and NUMBER represents the export control classification number. In this determination, the license types are determined by the active legal regulation, by the departure country for export, and by the destination country for import. The country group is picked based on the partner country in the document and classification assigned to the product.

Another important functionality is the content maintenance for ECCN, harmonized tariff number and commodity codes (see Figure 3.19). In SAP GTS edition for HANA, you have options to auto upload the content using an XML interface. You have to keep the content current, as the regulation updates the changes to the ECCN, HTS and commodity codes. SAP GTS edition for HANA also provides functionality to review the product that is impacted due to the new codes and provides functionality to replace the old codes with new ones.

Compliance checks are performed for export and import throughout the order cycle: sales order, fulfillment, and invoicing. Another key functionality with license is that you can determine license based on partner type. You can have multiple search strategies for license type determination. You can configure it to set up text determinations based on the license type (e. g., if the business has a requirement to print a particular text for a particular license type). In specific cases, for example, a special comprehensive li-

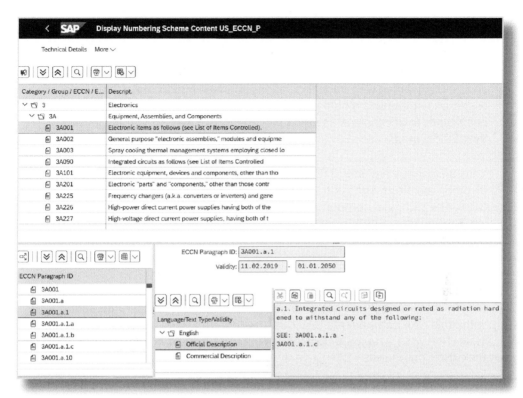

Figure 3.19: ECCN code numbering scheme maintained at subcategory level

cense, you might have a requirement to print special instructions on a trade document. While maintaining a license, the system allows you to maintain text, and you can choose to print that in the trade documents. You can set up the license type to track both quantity and value depreciation. The compliance functionality extends to import as well. The import checks can be performed throughout the purchasing cycle.

Another key functionality with GTS edition for HANA is the re-export check on relevant products. When you export product, it is not only important that you check the export regulation of the exporting country but also the country it is being shipped to. Furthermore, if this product is going to be re-shipped from the country receiving it (re-exported), the end destination of the product is also important. If the product is received into a country and the intent is to ship it to a different country after processing, then the re-export law of the originating country can still apply.

3.6.1 SAP GTS plug-in enhancements

The SAP GTS Plug-in software component allows businesses to integrate their ERP system with SAP GTS edition for HANA. This integration helps ensure compliance with trade regulations, manage import and export processes, and streamline global trade operations. The SAP GTS Plug-in allows businesses to access and use the functionality of SAP GTS without leaving their ERP system.

You can manage any SAP GTS upgrades and implementations independent of other functions and modules within the SAP ERP system (see Figure 3.20). The technical component is called SLL-PI (Legal and Logistics Plug-In). The advantage of this new plug-in is that you can upgrade the SAP GTS plug-in independent of the central plug-in and without having to upgrade the SAP ERP system.

If you are accessing the SAP GTS Plug-in from an SAP S/4 system the GTS plug-in customizing path has changed to a new location under integration with other SAP components SAP CUSTOMIZING IMPLEMENTATION GUIDE • INTEGRATION WITH OTHER SAP COMPONENTS • INTEGRATION WITH GOVERNANCE, RISK AND COMPLIANCE • SAP GLOBAL TRADE SERVICES.

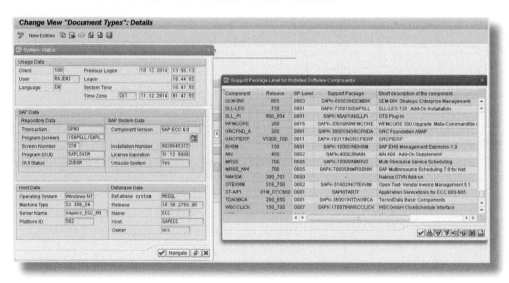

Figure 3.20: SAP GTS Plug-in in SAP S/4 system

The following are some of the new functionalities introduced in the latest SAP GTS Plug-in.

Advanced option to control the document transfer from SAP S/4 HANA ERP to SAP GTS

The new plug-in allows flexibility in transferring documents to SAP GTS. This option allows us to restrict specific order types at company code level from transferring to GTS. The following customizing option shows how this can be achieved (See Figure 3.21). Customizing access path SAP CUSTOMIZING IMPLEMENTATION GUIDE • INTEGRATION WITH OTHER SAP COMPONENTS • INTEGRATION WITH GOVERNANCE, RISK AND COMPLIANCE • SAP GLOBAL TRADE SERVICES • CONTROL DATA FOR TRANSFER TO SAP GLOBAL TRADE SERVICES • CONFIGURE CONTROL SETTINGS FOR DOCUMENT TRANSFER.

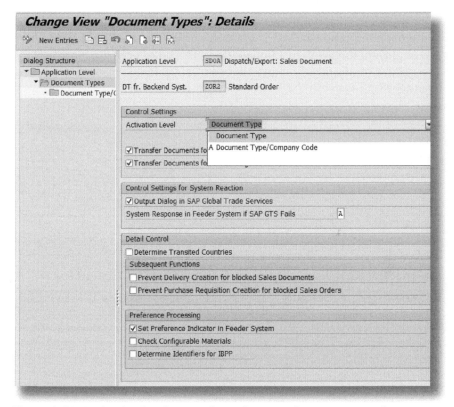

Figure 3.21: Activation level to restrict order types by company code

You can choose the ACTIVATION LEVEL at DOCUMENT TYPE or DOCUMENT TYPE/COMPANY CODE LEVEL. If you choose DOCUMENT TYPE/COMPANY CODE LEVEL, you can configure an individual company code for a document type (see Figure 3.22). In the example configuration setup below, order type ZOR2 for company code US01 will be sent to SAP GTS and UA01 will be skipped for GTS transfer.

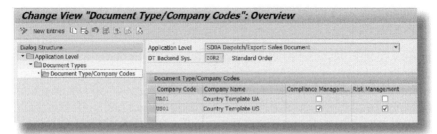

Figure 3.22: Selecting activation of service at company code level

Restrict subsequent functions due to GTS block

In the event of GTS order block, we should make sure the further actions for that order are blocked in SAP S/4 HANA system. We now have a standard way to prevent follow-on functionality for sales order from creating delivery or purchase requisition. You can choose to activate this by order type (see Figure 3.23).

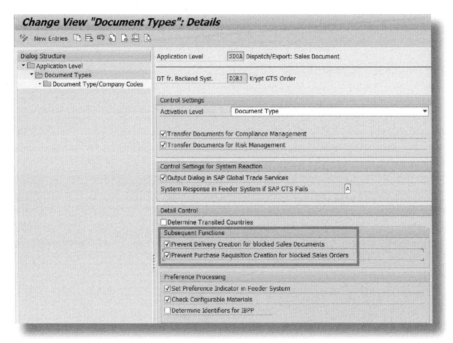

Figure 3.23: Activation to restrict follow-on functions

Export compliance check on outbound sales transactions based on routes

Following a compliance check and clearance, the system grants permission to create a declaration document, which is generated from the billing document. The recommended document type is the proforma billing type because the export compliance check might not just be checking against the departure country and the destination country. The shipment might pass through a third country before it finally reaches its destination. For example, a shipment sent to Germany might first land in Belgium, move to France, and finally reach Germany. SAP GTS edition for HANA allows you to perform export compliance checks based on the route the shipment takes. If the route includes an embargoed country, you may have to use a different route for the shipment. In some cases, it may be allowed with the appropriate license.

You can achieve legal control (license determination) by setting up route determination and turning on the indicator for it in SAP CUSTOMIZING IMPLEMENTATION GUIDE • INTEGRATION WITH OTHER SAP COMPONENTS • INTEGRATION WITH GOVERNANCE, RISK AND COMPLIANCE • SAP GLOBAL TRADE SERVICES • CONTROL DATA FOR TRANSFER TO SAP GLOBAL TRADE SERVICES • CONFIGURE CONTROL SETTINGS FOR DOCUMENT TRANSFER. Select the APPLICATION LEVEL (SD0A) and click DOCUMENT TYPES. Within the document type transfer configuration, select LEGAL CONTROL—DETERMINE TRANSITED COUNTRIES under DETAIL CONTROL (see Figure 3.24).

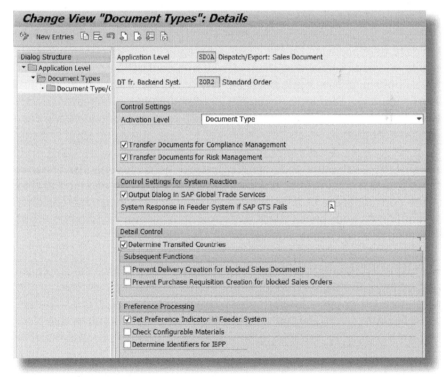

Figure 3.24: Export compliance service check based on route activation

> **! Choose desired check type**
>
> In Figure 3.24, the document type CALL UP SAP COMPLIANCE MANAGE-MENT SERVICES is selected. This enables a compliance check on the logistics transaction, or document type (ZOR2—Copy of Standard Order). If you select the check box under DETAIL CONTROL, the system performs a route check.

> **☛ What are documents?**
>
> Within the SAP system, key functions and activities are registered as *documents*. This could be a sales order for acknowledging the sales contract between a company and the customer or a purchase order contract for goods or services between a company and the vendor. **Documents** are the key to performing the compliance check from trade services for routes, hazardous substance checks, or inbound delivery import compliance checks.

Shipment consolidation

Typically, goods leaving for the same geographic locations are consolidated into one commercial document or customs declaration document. This helps companies save costs because they do not have to manage or track them separately. Proforma documents, created against the delivery document, trigger customs documents in SAP GTS for generating the trade declaration documents.

In SAP ERP, a shipment document is used for consolidating deliveries. In the past with a consolidated shipment, you needed to manage the tracking of the consolidation, or have the freight forwarder manage the customs declaration on your behalf. With proforma consolidation, customers used the billing due list (transaction VF04).

Billing due list referred the deliveries for consolidation. Once the shipment was created, the delivery documents had to be manually entered to the billing due list to generate the consolidated proforma. With the shipment consolidation option, you can simply enter the shipment number. This shipment number has all of the deliveries associated with it, helping you avoid any duplicate manual effort and error. Along with this, a shipment document also stores critical export data elements like mode of transport, carrier, export date, import date, ports and pass this information to SAP GTS to be reported to customs authorities.

Figure 3.25 shows the selection screen for creating a consolidated proforma based on the billing document, outbound delivery, shipment number, or load. In this example, the shipment consolidation transaction pulls the deliveries associated with the shipment and generates the consolidated proforma.

Shipment Consolidation: Generate Customs Declarations from Sales Docs			
BillingDoc			
Billing Type	F8 Pro Forma Inv f. Delivery ▼		
Billing Date			
Outb. Delivery			
Delivery		to	
Sales Organization		to	
Shipping Point/Receiving Pt		to	
Shipping Conditions		to	
Incoterms			
Delivery Group		to	
Pland Gds Mvmnt Date	24.02.2023	to	04.03.2023
Ship-to Party		to	
Destination Country/Region		to	
Forwarding Agent		to	
Shipment			
Shipment Number	1050	to	
Route		to	
Shipping Type		to	
Forwarding Agent		to	
Load			
Loading Point		to	
Door for Whse No.		to	
Layout			
Layout			
Background Processing			
☐ No Blocked Items			

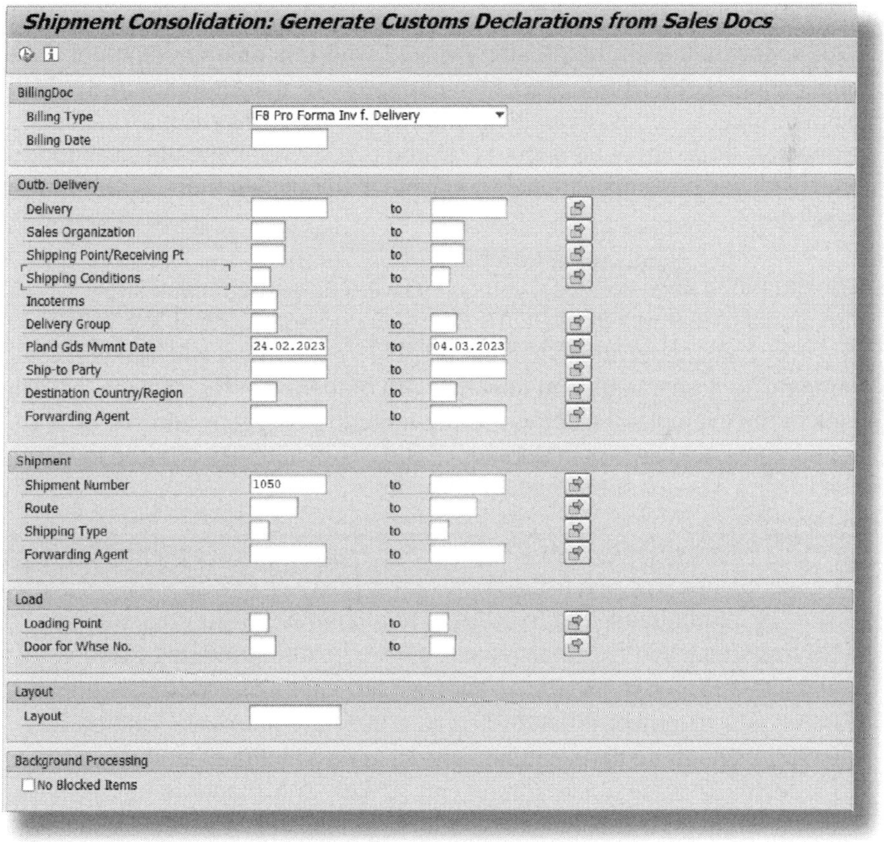

Figure 3.25: Shipment consolidation by shipment number

3.7 ITAR

Imagine a defense equipment manufacturing company wants to bid on the design of an equipment or control system that can be used in a missile or fighter jet. Before it can even engage on the bid and share specific product information, the US State Department requires the exporter to apply for a technical assistance agreement (TAA) to facilitate the sharing of information. The TAA operates similarly to a license, and you can designate it for a specific product, USML, customer, country, and so on.

When an exporter wants to ship physical goods out of the country, the company needs to apply for an export license, such as a DSP-5 (Permanent Export). The application for this license must reference the existing and valid TAA associated with the project involved with this sale or shipment. The application of the DSP-5 must take into account the attribute on the TAA such as dates, values, quantities, and so on. Temporary export for public exhibition, trade show, air show, or related event, even if the physical goods were licensed previously for public exhibition, requires a DSP-73 (temporary export).

For situations such as these, you can use the agreements and license type functionality features in SAP GTS Compliance Legal Control. We will show you the configuration steps to meet the ITAR requirement with license types referencing agreements and how they are managed in the system. We will look at the example of a defense manufacturing company and see how the agreements are used for initial export shipments and then referred to within the license type for subsequent shipments.

☛ ITAR

The US International Traffic in Arms Regulations (ITAR) stipulates that US importers and exporters must follow certain standards to operate with defense-related material and technologies. This includes the requirement to obtain different licenses based on the US Munition List (USML). The **three main categories of licenses** include hardware licenses, technical assistance agreements (TAA), and manufacture license agreements (MLA). Some cases call for multiple licenses across different processes.

3.7.1 Configuration steps

Let's review the configuration steps for ITAR.

Step 1: Define agreements. As explained in the scenarios above, the company will have to start the information sharing in terms of design document as a technical agreement. As a first step, we need to configure agreements. Follow menu path SPRO • SAP GLOBAL TRADE SERVICES, EDITION FOR SAP HANA • COMPLIANCE MANAGEMENT • LEGAL CONTROL • APPROVALS • DEFINE TYPES OF AGREEMENTS (see Figure 3.26). After you create an agreement, the system references it by the license type. While defining the agreement in the OBJECTS TO BE CHECKED section, you need to select attributes within the transaction that you need to validate before assigning the agreement to the document or transaction. Check the value and quantity and update the value and gross weight respectively. Also, make sure that you define a depreciation group to use in the agreement quantity and value update. To do so, follow the menu path SPRO • SAP GLOBAL TRADE SERVICES, EDITION FOR SAP HANA • COMPLIANCE MANAGEMENT • LEGAL CONTROL • APPROVALS • DEFINE DEPRECIATION GROUP IN AGREEMENTS. Once there, create a name and description for the depreciation group. The depreciation group helps to accumulate the value and quantity depreciation. Once defined, it needs to be assigned in the agreement definition.

👉 Agreements vs. licenses in SAP GTS edition for HANA

Agreements are a specific requirement for ITAR controls. You will not need this functionality to manage licenses for some other controls such as the Export Administration Regulations (EAR). An ITAR Technical Assistance Agreement (TAA) is the overarching agreement between your organization and the Department of State Defense Trade Controls (DTC). This agreement will control everything from what you are manufacturing to your sharing of product details with foreign nationals. It will also govern your permission to export. Note that you will still generally need to get a transactional license for each shipment. Think of the TAA as blanket permission (it may state that you can sell 100 units of a controlled product per year). Each transactional license will also have a quantity limit, and the sum total of each license must not exceed your TAA. GTS will link the licenses to the TAA and monitor this for you.

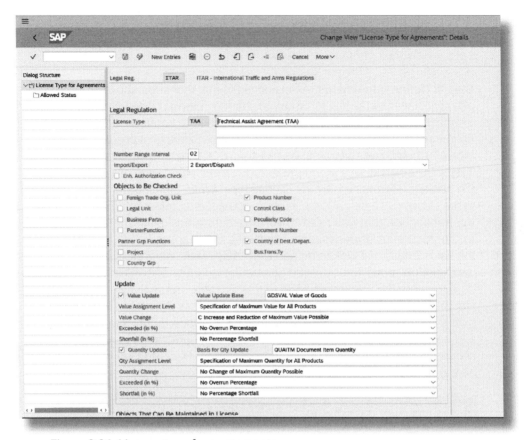

Figure 3.26: License type for agreements

Step 2: Define license type and assign agreement. ITAR uses temporary and permanent licenses and as explained, we might have to refer these licenses to the previous agreement. *License type* defines the attributes that you would like to have in the license. To define the license type, you need to select the object to be checked, value, and quantity to update. Follow menu path SPRO • SAP GLOBAL TRADE SERVICES, EDITION FOR SAP HANA • COMPLIANCE MANAGEMENT • LEGAL CONTROL • APPROVALS • DEFINE IMPORT- AND EXPORT LICENSE TYPES to display the license type definition. The definitions of attributes appear when you create licenses. When you scroll down in the license type definition, you need to assign the agreement type to the license types. Figure 3.27 and Figure 3.28 display the agreement assignment to license types.

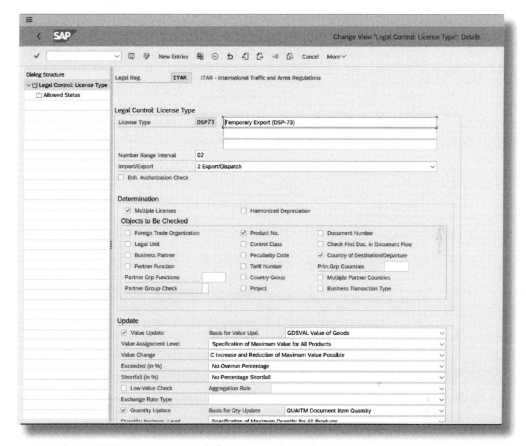

Figure 3.27: License type definitions with attributes

In the AGREEMENT tab, make sure you assign the TYPE OF AGREEMENT and DEPRECIATION GROUP you created in Step 1.

GTS data setups: The steps noted above explained the configurations to set up the agreements and license types. In the next step, we will go over the master data set up that is required for this function to work.

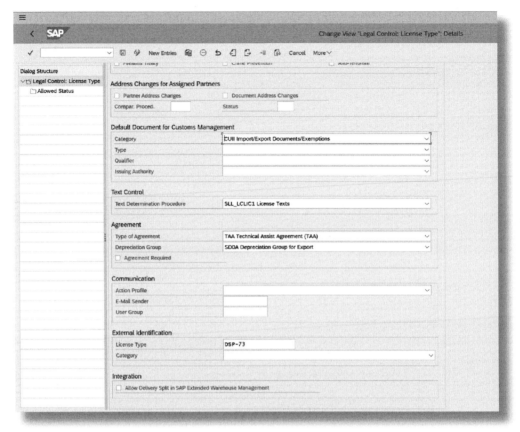

Figure 3.28: Assignment of agreement and depreciation group to license type

Step 3: Build your determination strategy. Following the agreement and license type definition, you need to build the license type determination table. In the license determination, maintain the search logic for license type and agreement determination based on the determination procedure. For example, the license type is determined based on the departure country, destination country, trouping, and USML (Number). Launch FIORI LAUNCHPAD find app MAINTAIN DETERMINATION STRATEGY under group LICENSE MANAGEMENT. Build the table against the license type and agreement (**AGREM**) based on the grouping for hardware and technical agreement for the respective classification number. Figure 3.29 shows the table that displays the legal regulation, grouping, departure country, classification number, and license type based on the license type determination procedure you defined.

Under CRITERIA, select LEGAL REGULATION, GROUPING, COUNTRIES (DESTINATION FOR EXPORT), NUMBER (USML), and the relevant license type. Click on COPY INDIVIDUALLY and you will see the entries appear under TIME SERIES.

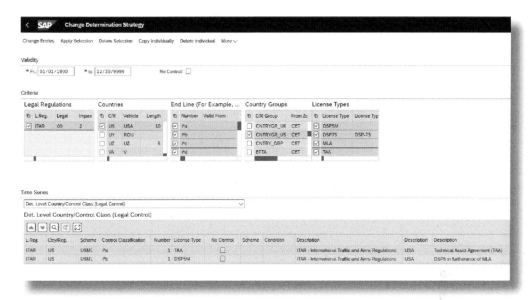

Figure 3.29: License type determination strategies by grouping for license type and agreement

Step 4: Create agreements. In the FIORI Launchpad find app MAINTAIN AGREEMENTS under LEGAL CONTROL and ITAR section or find the app using the search option (see Figure 3.30). Based on the agreement defined in the configuration in Step 1, you can maintain the agreements here.

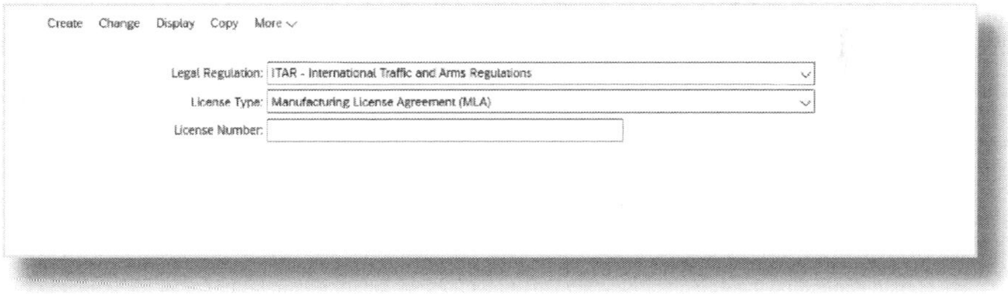

Figure 3.30: Create agreement based on the legal regulation and license type

When you click on CREATE AGREEMENT, it will bring up the screen shown in Figure 3.31 showing the details behind the agreement when it is created. As you can see, based on the attributes selected in Step 1, they appear when you create the agreement, value, quantity, control classes, and country of departure/destination.

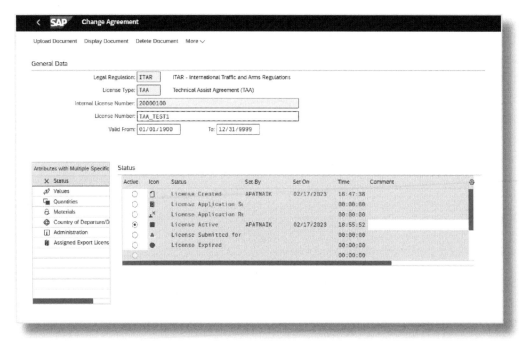

Figure 3.31: Agreement created with status active and other attributes as defined in configuration

Step 5: Create licenses. Once you have an agreement in place, you can create licenses. When you create the license with the agreement assigned in the configuration, it is required to reference the agreement. A license can be created using FIORI app MANAGE LICENSES which can be found under the LEGAL CONTROL section. When you create a license for the license type defined in Step 2 of the configuration, the system asks for an agreement reference (see Figure 3.32). You will have to enter the legal regulation and license type and select the agreement type and agreement number that you want to assign to this license from the drop-down menu.

You can use an agreement created in Step 4 in the agreement reference to create a license. After you enter the details in the field shown in Figure 3.3 and click CONTINUE, it will bring up the screen shown in Figure 3.33. You need to fill in the EXTERNAL LICENSE NUMBER based on the license approval received and the VALID FROM and VALID TO. The value and quantity are derived from the agreement and should not exceed the agreement quantity and values. Within the control, you maintain the USML number and Country of Dept/Destination, and destination country. The status maintains the audit of the license when it was created, when it was applied for, and active or expired information.

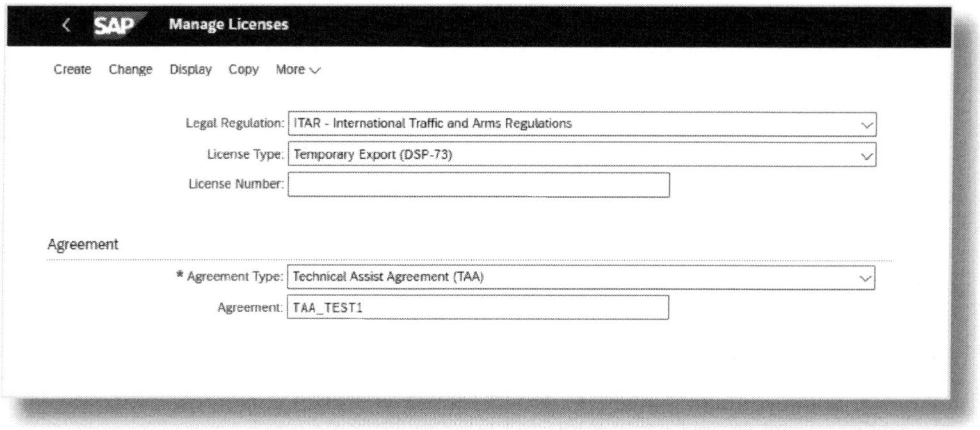

Figure 3.32: Create license with agreement reference

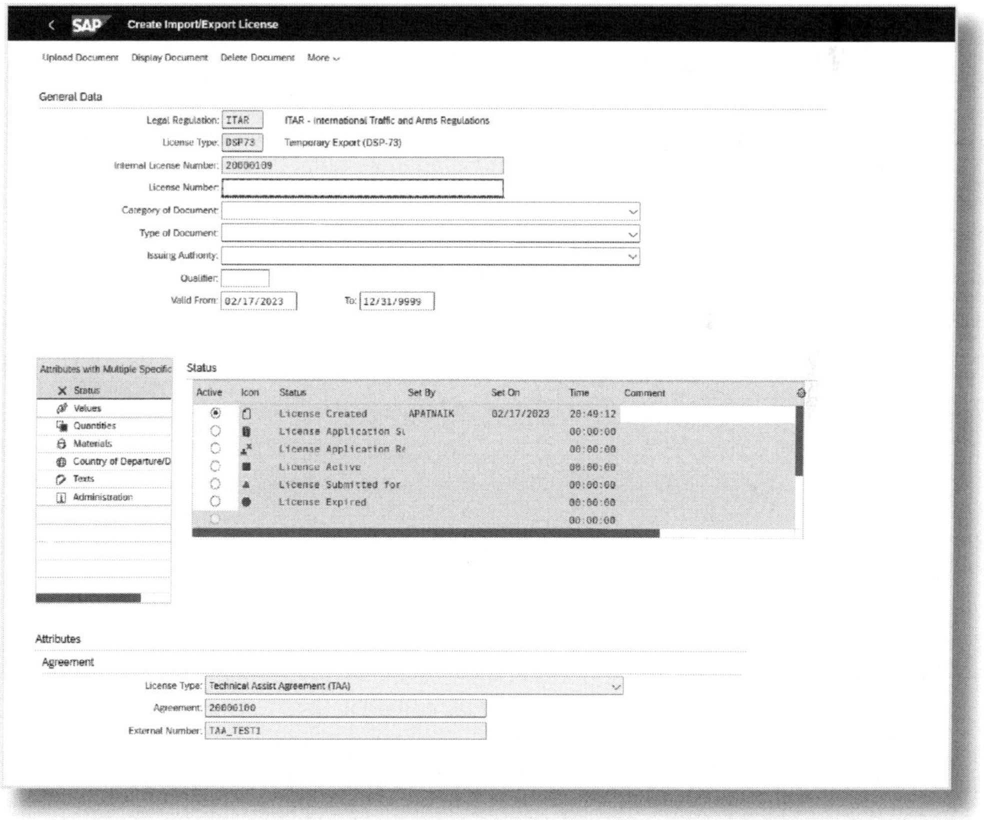

Figure 3.33: License display with agreement referenced

You can create an agreement with reference to another license type or agreement. When you display the agreement, you can see the license type that is assigned to the agreement, and in the center, with the details of License Type, License Number, Ext. No., Valid from, and Valid to. Figure 3.34 displays the license type assigned to the agreement. This can be accessed using the FIORI APP MANAGE LICENSES which can be found under LEGAL CONTROL and CLICK ON DISPLAY.

Figure 3.34: License assignment to document

Step 6: Classify and group the product. You need to assign material or products with the classification number (USML). These classification numbers and grouping in turn determine the license and agreement based on the license determination strategy you maintained in Step 3. Open the FIORI APP MANAGE PRODUCTS under compliance MASTER DATA and click on CHANGE. While you are here, you need to assign the USML classification in the export classification number and grouping (see Figure 3.35). You can search for the number and group from the drop-down list.

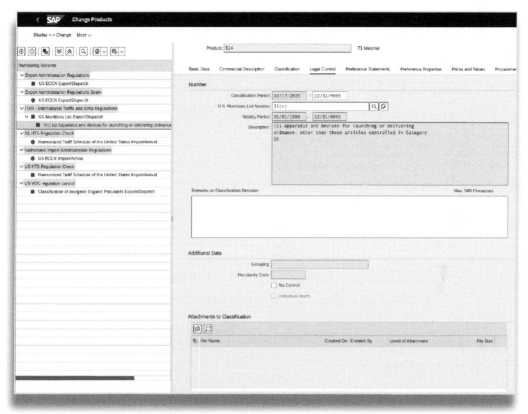

Figure 3.35: Change products (ITAR)

Step 7: Assign transaction of the agreement and license. Based on the configuration setting and GTS cockpit setting, when you create the sales order, you assign a license type and agreement. Figure 3.26 displays the log in SAP GTS following the sales order being saved in ECC. The document assignment to the agreement and license can be found using FIORI APP DISPLAY ASSIGNED DOCUMENTS under the LEGAL CONTROL—LICENSE MANAGEMENT section. You can use the sales order number in the REFERENCE NUMBER field and click on execute. In the report, if you click on the log, it will bring up the screen shown in Figure 3.36.

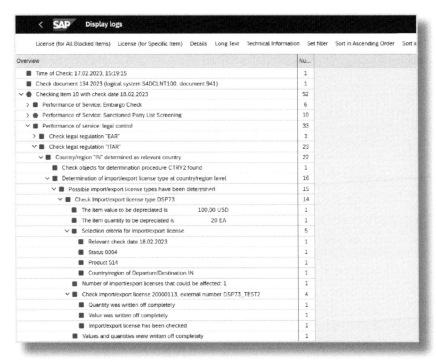

Figure 3.36: Display log

The first line item displays the license type assignment based on the legal regulation, destination country from the document, and the classification and grouping assigned to the product in **Step 7**.

Now that we have seen the document with the agreement and license type assigned, let's go back to the agreement and license type display and view the updates there.

When you display the license (see Figure 3.37), you can see the value and the quantity written off as seen in the display log. Use the FIORI APP MANAGE AGREEMENTS AND CLICK ON DISPLAY.

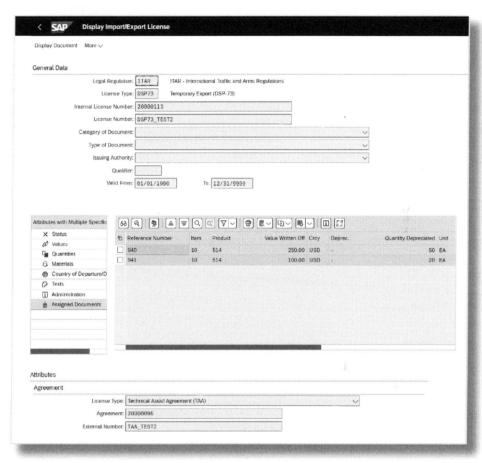

Figure 3.37: Display import/export license

Let's look at the updates to the license. Open FIORI APP MANAGE LICENSE •
CLICK ON DISPLAY (see Figure 3.38 and Figure 3.39).

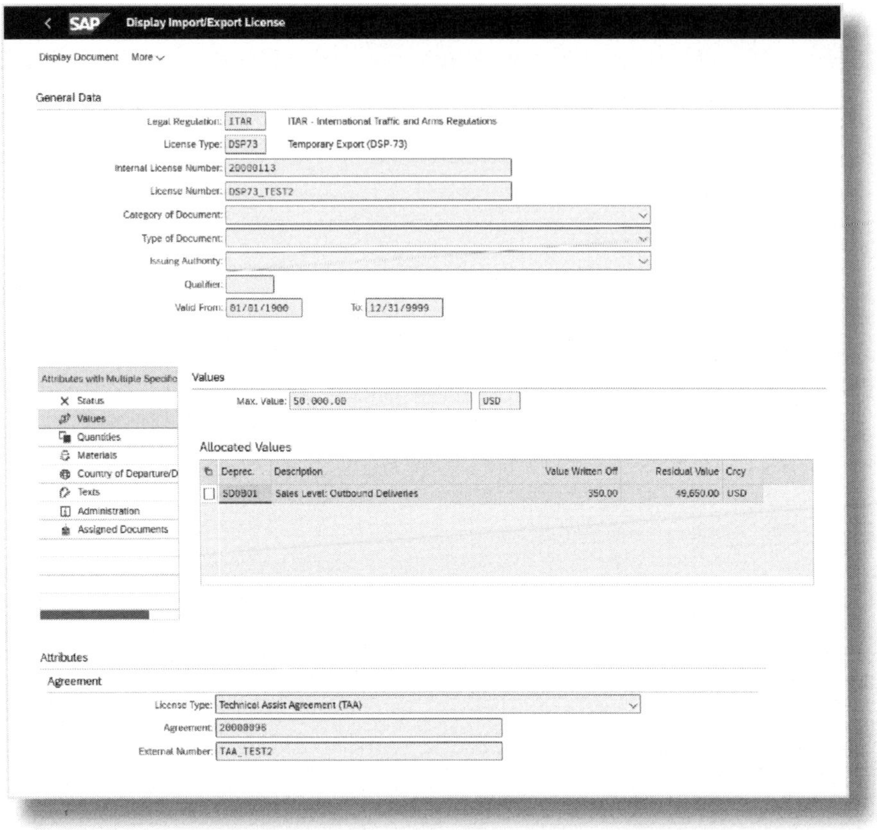

Figure 3.38: Display license (value allocated)

To summarize, we created an agreement and assigned licenses to the
agreement. We then classified the product. When the product was used in
a sales order, based on the departure and destination country, it picked up
the appropriate license and agreement. We might have gotten an agreement for a technical agreement, and when the actual product was shipped,
we were able to refer to that. The display log showed the agreement, the
license assignment, and the depreciated value and quantity. Once we saw
the transaction assignment, we also confirmed the update to the license
and agreement. Agreement values are decreased based on the licenses
assigned, and license value and quantity are decreased based on the transaction.

Figure 3.39: Display license (quantity allocated)

3.8   Domestic state level compliance check

In this section we will see how to activate any domestic order control. We will use an example of US state level control check for Volatile Organic Compound (VOC) Control Regulations. Regarding this regulation, we must track items that are allowed to be sold or stored according to a particular US state's thresholds and laws. We can use SAP GTS legal control framework to achieve complete control of shipping and tracking order quantities shipping such products.

Step 1: Define a new legal regulation for domestic check

In this step, define a legal regulation for the hazardous substance check (see Figure 3.40). The menu path is SPRO.SAP GLOBAL TRADE SERVICES, EDITION FOR SAP HANA • GENERAL SETTINGS • LEGAL REGULATIONS • DEFINE LEGAL REGULATIONS.

Figure 3.40: Define legal regulation

Within the TYPE OF LEGAL CODE, select PROHIBITION AND RESTRICTION from the drop-down menu and select EXPORT/DISPATCH from the IMPORT/EXPORT indicator. Key in the original country of legal regulation.

Step 2: Activate the legal regulations at the country/country group level (see Figure 3.41).

The menu path is SPRO.SAP GLOBAL TRADE SERVICES, EDITION FOR SAP HANA • GENERAL SETTINGS • LEGAL REGULATIONS • ACTIVATE LEGAL REGULATIONS AT COUNTRY/COUNTRY GROUP LEVEL.

Figure 3.41: Activate legal regulation.

Step 3: Activate the legal regulations at legal control level for the country activated in previous step 2 at country/country group level (see Figure 3.42). Select CHECK: DISPATCH(EXCLUSIVELY) to check for only domestic transactions.

The menu path is SPRO.SAP GLOBAL TRADE SERVICES, EDITION FOR SAP HANA • COMPLIANCE MANAGEMENT • LEGAL CONTROLS • ACTIVATE LEGAL RE-GULATIONS.

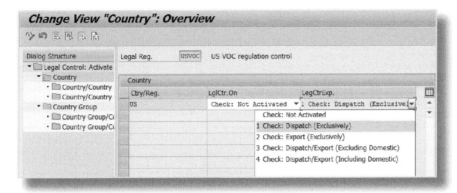

Figure 3.42: Legal regulation activation by country

Step 4: Create a new determination procedure for exclusively activating legal control check at region level (see Figure 3.43). Create a new entry and add new Assignment of determination strategy with SEQUENCE NUMBER = 10 AND DETERMINATION STRATEGY = CD20 AT REGION/REGION/CONTROL CLASS

The menu path is SPRO.SAP GLOBAL TRADE SERVICES, EDITION FOR SAP HANA • COMPLIANCE MANAGEMENT • LEGAL CONTROLS • DEFINE DETERMINA-TION PROCEDURE TO AUTOMATICALLY DETERMINE LICENSE TYPES.

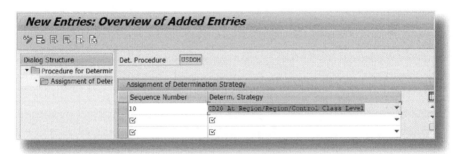

Figure 3.43: Create new determination procedure

Step 5: Legal regulation created in Step 2 we need to setup control settings. Select PRODUCT MASTER MAINTENANCE to B ONLY SPECIFICALLY SELECTED PRODUCTS ARE RELEVANT FOR CHECKS; LICENSE TYPE DET. PROCEDURE as domestic procedure defined in Step 4. Other parameters you can choose as required in the recommended setup are selected (see Figure 3.44).

The menu path is SPRO.SAP GLOBAL TRADE SERVICES, EDITION FOR SAP HANA • COMPLIANCE MANAGEMENT • LEGAL CONTROLS • CONTROL SETTINGS FOR LEGAL CONTROL.

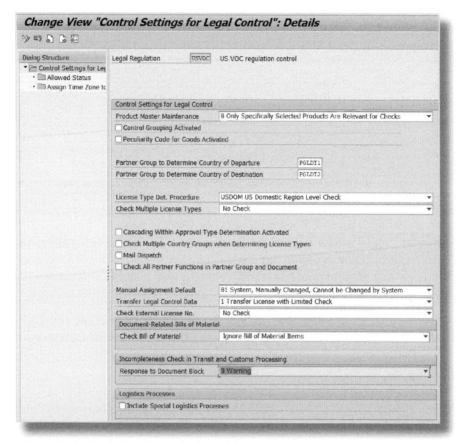

Figure 3.44: Control settings for Legal Control

👉 Recommended setting for a new legal regulation

When setting up a new legal regulation when the GTS system is already live, choose the product maintenance as "Specifically selected products are relevant checks." This means that when regulation is active in production it will not cause disruption to order flow and only required products can be activated for the regulation.

Step 6: Create a control list number for this regulation. We could create our own list for various classifications for inorganic pollutant, for example: VOCV—Very volatile (gaseous) organic compounds, VOCS—Semi volatile organic compounds and VOCC—Volatile organic compounds.

The menu path is SPRO.SAP Global Trade Services, edition for SAP HANA · General Settings · Numbering Schemes · Control Classes.

The following three steps are required:

1. Define Numbering Scheme for Control Classes. See Figure 3.45.

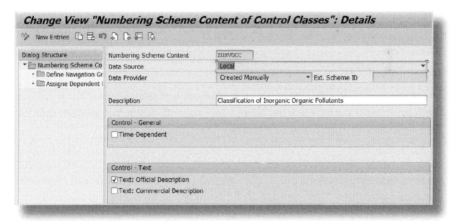

Figure 3.45: Create a new number scheme.

2. Define Numbering Scheme Content for Control Classes. See Figure 3.46.

Figure 3.46: Create a numbering scheme content to manually maintain the classification.

3. Activate Numbering Scheme Content for Control Classes. See Figure 3.47.

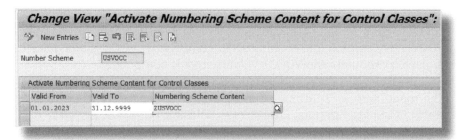

Figure 3.47: Assign the numbering scheme content to numbering scheme

Step 7: Maintain license types that are to be allow based on the approved products to ship or by approved customers or a one-time exception license. See Figure 3.48

The menu path is SPRO.SAP GLOBAL TRADE SERVICES, EDITION FOR SAP HANA • COMPLIANCE MANAGEMENT • LEGAL CONTROLS • APPROVALS • DEFINE IMPORT- AND EXPORT LICENSE TYPES.

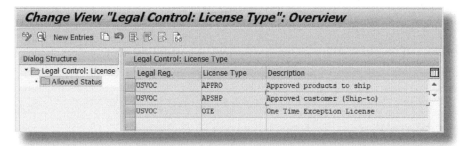

Figure 3.48: Create license types

Configuration is complete from Step 1 to 7 now we have to maintain master data by launching the FIORI launchpad

Step 8: Under control classes find tile "manage control classes" select number scheme content created in step 6 (see Figure 3.46) and maintain Inorganic pollutant main header and the values below (see Figure 3.49)

- ▶ VOCV—Very volatile (gaseous) organic compounds,
- ▶ VOCS—Semi volatile organic compounds
- ▶ VOCC—Volatile organic compounds

Access app MANAGE NUMBERING SCHEME CONTENT found under CONTROL CLASSES GROUP—MANAGE CONTROL CLASSES see below Figure 3.49

Figure 3.49: Maintain content for VOC classification

Step 9: Define determination strategy to control by ship-to and ship-from states. In the following example the determination is controlled for all states shipping to California and products classified as VOCC and has the option for all three licenses

Access app MANAGE DETERMINATION STRATEGY found under LICENSE MANAGEMENT block. See Figure 3.50.

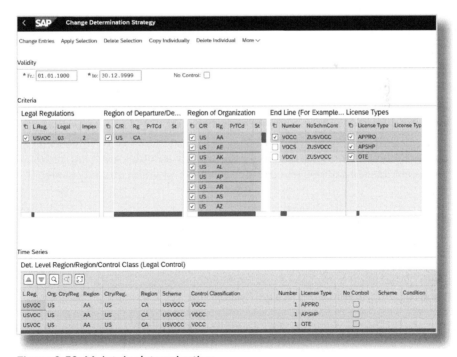

Figure 3.50: Maintain determination

Step 10: Classify and activate products that are controlled for VOC regulation. We have created three classifications of VOC product based on the fact that specific controls can be configured as per state regulation. Example: If very volatile (classification VOCV) may not be allowed to ship regularly but can be released based on a one-time exception. See below Figure 3.51.

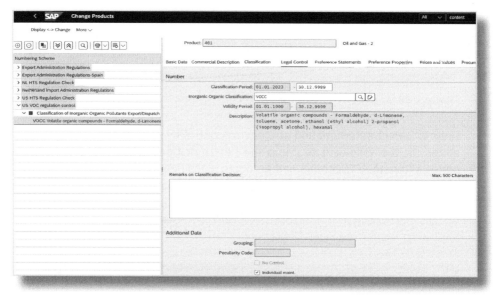

Figure 3.51: Classification for regulation VOC

Step 11: Orders shipping for this VOC controlled product to ship-to address in California will be blocked and referred out for the correct license. In this example the licenses are setup for product based, ship-to customer and one time exception. These licenses can also be configured to track value and/ or quantity shipped. See below Figure 3.52 for an order audit log showing different license options as configured in determination strategy in step 9.

3.9 SAP TM Integration

The integration between SAP GTS edition for HANA and TM allows the exchange of key data between the two modules, enabling real-time visibility into global trade compliance and logistics operations. Some of the key benefits of integrating SAP GTS and TM include:

▶ Improved visibility: By integrating GTS and TM, organizations can gain real-time visibility into global trade compliance and logistics operations, enabling them to make informed decisions and optimize their supply chain operations.

Overview	Nu...
■ Time of Check: 07.02.2023, 20:40:41	1
■ Check document 117 2023 (logical system S4DCLNT100, document 931)	1
∨ ● Checking item 10 with check date 08.02.2023	97
> ● Performance of Service: Embargo Check	10
> ■ Performance of Service: Sanctioned Party List Screening	28
∨ ● Performance of service: legal control	52
> ● Check legal regulation "EAR"	21
> ■ Check legal regulation "USHTS"	3
∨ ● Check legal regulation "USVOC"	27
∨ ● Country/region "US" determined as relevant country	26
■ Check objects for determination procedure USDOM found	1
∨ ● Determ. Imp/Exp License Type at Layer Region/Region/Control Class	24
∨ ● Possible import/export license types have been determined	23
> ● Check import/export license type APPRO	7
> ● Check import/export license type APSHP	7
> ● Check import/export license type OTE	8

Figure 3.52: Audit log for legal regulation USVOC blocked for material activated for this check

▶ Streamlined processes: Integrating GTS and TM helps to streamline processes and eliminate redundant data entry, reducing errors and improving efficiency.

▶ Enhanced compliance: The integration of GTS and TM helps organizations to stay compliant with global trade regulations, avoiding costly fines and penalties. It helps report accurate and up-to-date information to customs authorities.

▶ Better customer service: By integrating GTS and TM, organizations can improve customer service by providing accurate and timely information about shipments and delivery schedules.

SAP GTS edition for HANA now introduces the option to perform compliance checks at freight order level. Figure 3.53 below shows how SAP ECC, SAP TM and SAP GTS interact. The following prerequisites are necessary to enable the outbound process using and SAP TM and SAP GTS:

▶ Technical connections between SAP ERP, SAP TM and SAP GTS.

▶ Connections between SAP TM and SAP GTS can be established using SAP PI and corresponding delivered SOA services need to be set up.

▶ Master Data Replication from SAP ERP to SAP GTS—Material Master / Customer Master.

▶ Master Data Replication from SAP ERP to SAP TM—Organizational Data / Customer Master / Material Master.

▶ Customizing settings belonging to the business processes in SAP ERP, SAP TM and SAP GTS

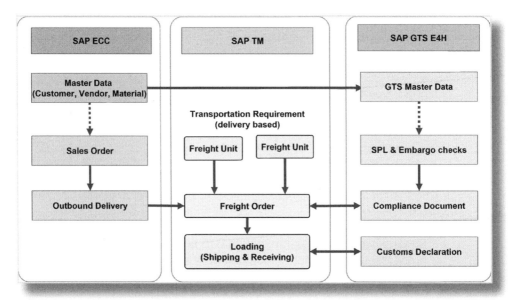

Figure 3.53: TM—SAP GTS Integration

Following SOA services need to be setup

SAP TM—SAP GTS integration leverages service-oriented architecture (SOA) services. SOA middleware facilitates communication between different applications or systems based on the exchange of XML messages. SOA helps in the integration by using Web services to design business solutions to meet ever evolving business needs quickly. Figure 3.54 shows the various sender and receiver services that need to be activated.

ExportDeclarationSUITERequest—Service to enable SAP TM to create customs export declarations in SAP GTS.

ExportDeclarationSUITECancellationRequest—To cancel customs export declarations out of SAP TM these services are used.

From Sender SOA Service	To Receiver SOA Service
Name: ExportDeclarationSUITERequest_Out **Namespace:** http://sap.com/xi/TMS/Global **System:** SAP TM	**Name:** ExportDeclarationSUITERequest_In **Namespace:** http://sap.com/xi/GTS/Global2 **System:** SAP GTS
Name: ExportDeclarationSUITECancellationRequest_Out **Namespace:** http://sap.com/xi/TMS/Global **System:** SAP TM	**Name:** ExportDeclarationSUITECancellationRequest_In **Namespace:** http://sap.com/xi/GTS/Global2 **System:** SAP GTS
Name: ExportDeclarationSUITEConfirmation_Out **Namespace:** http://sap.com/xi/GTS/Global2 **System:** SAP GTS	**Name:** ExportDeclarationSUITEConfirmation_In **Namespace:** http://sap.com/xi/TMS/Global **System:** SAP TM
Name: TradeComplianceCheckSUITERequest_Out **Namespace:** http://sap.com/xi/TMS/Global **System:** SAP TM	**Name:** TradeComplianceCheckSUITERequest_In **Namespace:** http://sap.com/xi/GTS/Global2 **System:** SAP GTS
Name: TradeComplianceCheckSUITEConfirmation_Out **Namespace:** http://sap.com/xi/GTS/Global2 **System:** SAP GTS	**Name:** TradeComplianceCheckSUITEConfirmation_In **Namespace:** http://sap.com/xi/TMS/Global **System:** SAP TM

Figure 3.54: SOA Services

ExportDeclarationSUITEConfirmation—Sending status information out of SAP GTS (e.g., release of customs export declaration ITN) is handled by this service.

TradeComplianceCheckSUITERequest—Request a trade compliance check for a transportation business document.

TradeComplianceCheckSUITEConfirmation—Share the compliance status based on the compliance check from SAP GTS to SAP TM.

SAP TM Configuration

Enable compliance check flag at the freight order level. This will trigger the SAP GTS compliance checks for the freight orders.

Follow the configuration path SPRO • SAP CUSTOMIZING IMPLEMENTATION GUIDE • TRANSPORTATION MANAGEMENT • FREIGHT ORDER MANAGEMENT • FREIGHT ORDER • DEFINE FREIGHT ORDER TYPES (see Figure 3.55).

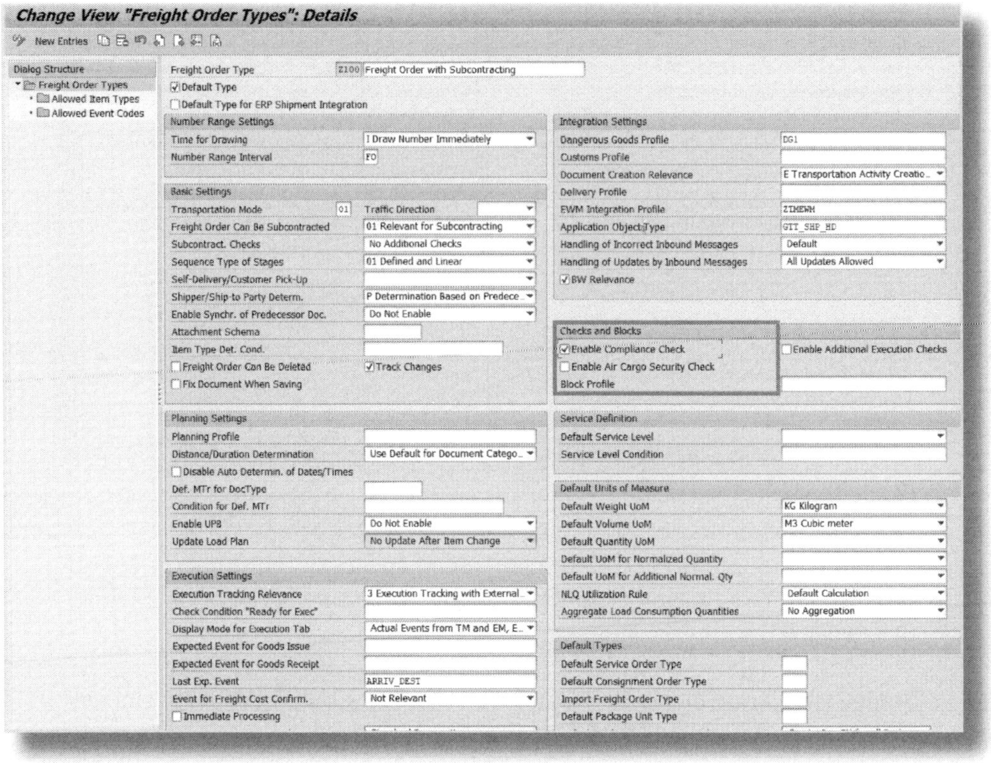

Figure 3.55: Enable Freight Order for Compliance check

Define and assign customs activity and profile at Freight order and Freight booking level. A customs activity contains settings that control customs handling for a specific process (for example, export or transit), grouping strategy for items to be consolidated and customs declaration trigger status. Follow the configuration path SPRO • SAP CUSTOMIZING IMPLEMENTATION GUIDE • TRANSPORTATION MANAGEMENT • BASIC FUNCTIONS • GLOBAL TRADE • DEFINE CUSTOMS ACTIVITIES AND PROFILES (see Figure 3.56 and Figure 3.57). After defining customs activity and profile, assign the customs activity to the profile created as the last step in this process.

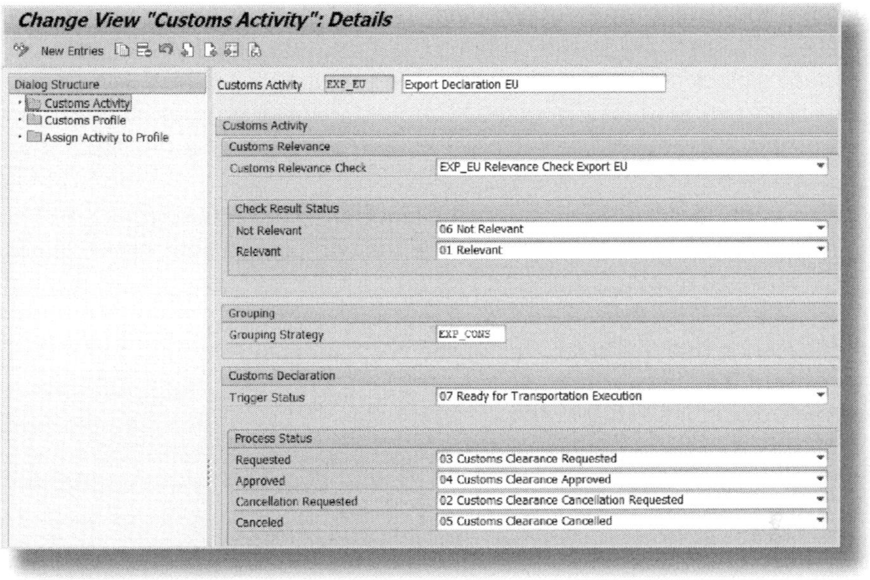

Change View "Customs Activity": Details

New Entries

Dialog Structure
• Customs Activity
• Customs Profile
• Assign Activity to Profile

Customs Activity   EXP_EU   Export Declaration EU

Customs Activity

Customs Relevance

Customs Relevance Check	EXP_EU Relevance Check Export EU

Check Result Status

Not Relevant	06 Not Relevant
Relevant	01 Relevant

Grouping

Grouping Strategy	EXP_CONS

Customs Declaration

Trigger Status	07 Ready for Transportation Execution

Process Status

Requested	03 Customs Clearance Requested
Approved	04 Customs Clearance Approved
Cancellation Requested	02 Customs Clearance Cancellation Requested
Canceled	05 Customs Clearance Cancelled

Figure 3.56: Define Customs Activity

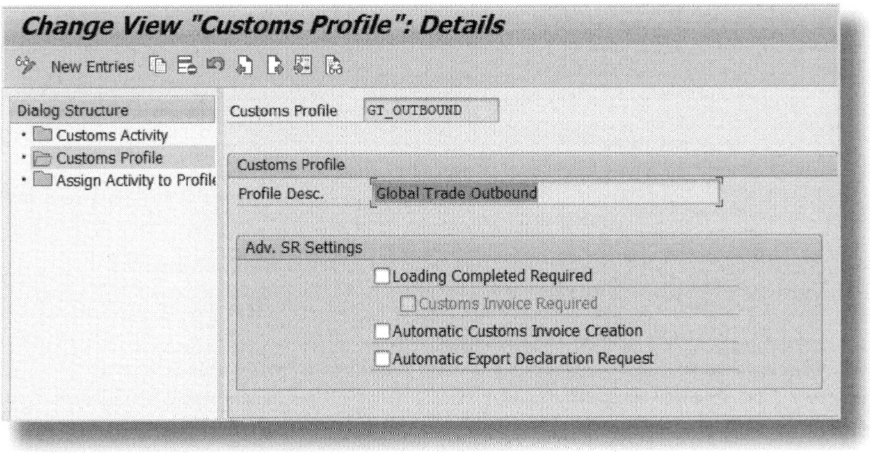

Change View "Customs Profile": Details

New Entries

Dialog Structure
• Customs Activity
• Customs Profile
• Assign Activity to Profile

Customs Profile   GT_OUTBOUND

Customs Profile

Profile Desc.	Global Trade Outbound

Adv. SR Settings

☐ Loading Completed Required
☐ Customs Invoice Required
☐ Automatic Customs Invoice Creation
☐ Automatic Export Declaration Request

Figure 3.57: Define Customs Profile

Define block reason codes and assign them to processes. If a defined block reason is set in a business document in SAP TM, the corresponding processes for this document are blocked. You can use manual block reasons to block processes in SAP TM for many types of objects. For example, you can block a forwarding order for planning. SAP TM also has block reasons that are set automatically by the system. The approval workflow is an example of such a block reason. Follow customizing setup SPRO • SAP CUSTOMIZING IMPLEMENTATION GUIDE • TRANSPORTATION MANAGEMENT • BASIC FUNCTIONS • GENERAL SETTINGS • DEFINE BLOCK REASON CODES (see Figure 3.58).

COMPLIANCE CHECK REQUIRED: A compliance check is required for a SAP TM business document when the result of the compliance screening has not been received from the SAP GTS system.

COMPLIANCE CHECK FAILED: The business document is blocked in SAP GTS due to a compliance check service.

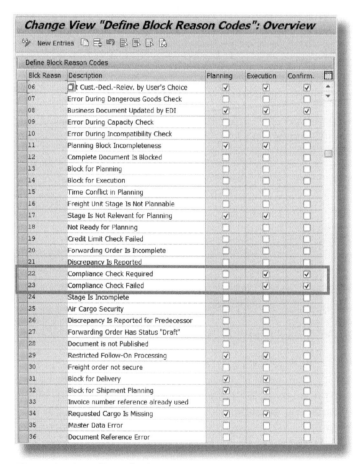

Figure 3.58: Define Block Reason

SAP GTS Configuration

Configuration on the GTS side starts with organizational structure mapping. Partner number used in SAP TM is mapped to the corresponding foreign trade organization in SAP GTS, at the feeder system level or the feeder system group level. Follow the customizing path SPRO • SAP GLOBAL TRADE SERVICES, EDITION FOR SAP HANA • GENERAL SETTINGS • ORGANIZATIONAL STRUCTURES • ASSIGNMENT OF ORGANIZATIONAL UNITS FROM FEEDER SYSTEM TO FOREIGN TRADE ORG.• ASSIGN PARTNER NUMBER AT FEEDER SYSTEM GROUP LEVEL.

See Figure 3.59 for the use of the predefined business partner role "0" to assign the organization ID to the corresponding foreign trade organization. External Partner number represents the SAP TM business partner number assigned to the company code. This is mapped to the corresponding foreign trade organization defined in SAP GTS.

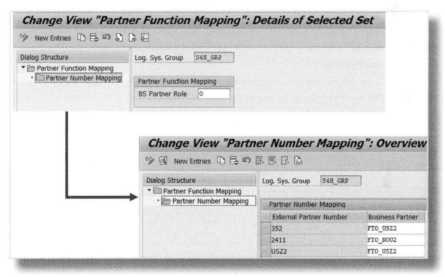

Figure 3.59: SAP TM—SAP GTS Organization unit mapping

Map the partner number from SAP TM to the corresponding legal unit in define in SAP GTS. Follow the customizing path SPRO • SAP GLOBAL TRADE SERVICES, EDITION FOR SAP HANA • GENERAL SETTINGS • ORGANIZATIONAL STRUCTURES • ASSIGNMENT OF ORGANIZATIONAL UNITS FROM FEEDER SYSTEM TO LEGAL UNIT • ASSIGN PARTNER NUMBER AT FEEDER SYSTEM GROUP LEVEL.

See Figure 3.60 to map the predefined business partner role "35" to the corresponding legal unit parameter and assign the external partner number from SAP TM to the corresponding Legal unit deified in SAP GTS.

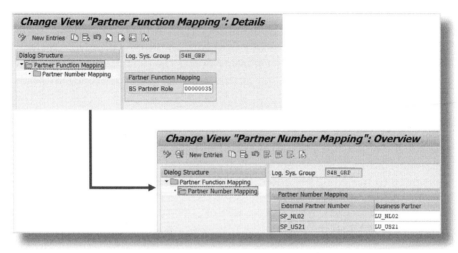

Figure 3.60: SAP TM—SAP GTS Legal unit mapping

You must assign partner functions in SAP GTS to partner functions in SAP TM at feeder system level or feeder system group level. Follow the customizing path SPRO • SAP GLOBAL TRADE SERVICES, EDITION FOR SAP HANA • GENERAL SETTINGS • PARTNER STRUCTURES • ASSIGNMENT OF PARTNER FUNCTIONS FROM FEEDER SYSTEMS • ASSIGN PARTNER FUNCTION AT FEEDER SYSTEM GROUP LEVEL (see Figure 3.61).

New Entries: Overview of Added Entries

New Entries

Mapping: Partner Function in FS Group to SAP GTS Part. Func.

Logical System ...	BS Partner Role	PartnerFunction	Description	Excl. Partn.Role	
S4H_GRP	1	AG	Sold To Party	☐	
S4H_GRP	10	RE	Bill-to Party	☐	
S4H_GRP	12	SP	Fwd. Agent	☐	
S4H_GRP	5	WE	Ship-to Party	☐	
S4H_GRP	8	RG	Payer	☐	

Figure 3.61: Assign partner function from SAP TM to SAP GTS

To assign the packaging material types of SAP TM to package types in SAP GTS follow the configuration path SPRO • SAP GLOBAL TRADE SERVICES, EDITION FOR SAP HANA • CUSTOMS MANAGEMENT • CUSTOMS CODE LISTS • ASSIGNMENT OF PACKAGING MATERIAL TYPES FROM FEEDER SYSTEMS.

Figure 3.62 shows that the mapping can be done at feeder system level or feeder system group level.

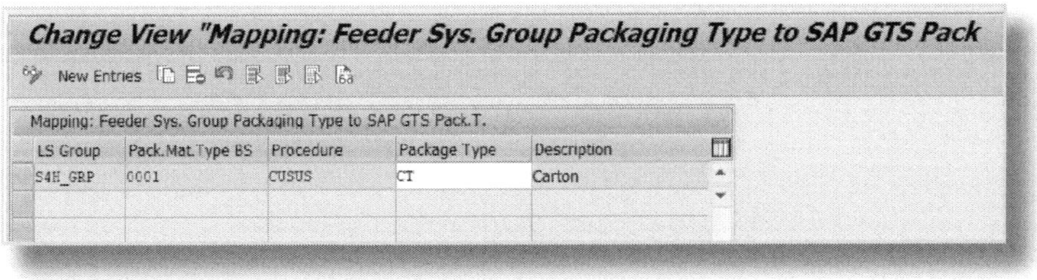

Figure 3.62: SAP TM and SAP GTS Packaging type mapping

SAP GTS determines the document type and the corresponding item category automatically, based on the activity sequence for the trade lane in SAP GTS. The introduction of a new document type in SAP GTS edition for HANA for mapping SAP TM order integration is shown below in Figure 3.63.

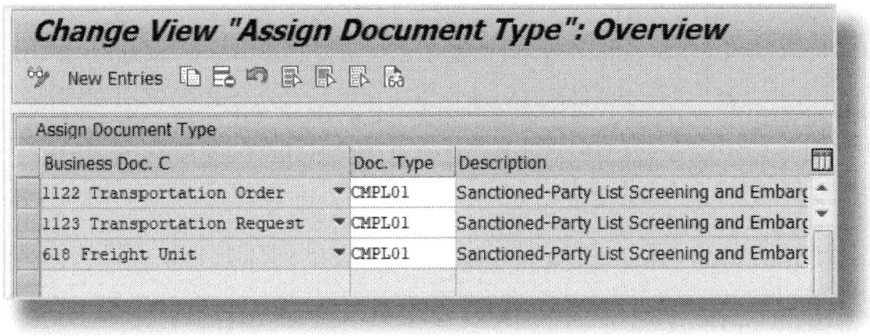

Figure 3.63: SAP TM Order mapping to SAP GTS document type

3.10 Examples of daily user functions in compliance

This section reviews several common daily user functions in the GTS compliance area. This list is not meant to be a comprehensive review of all available functions; rather, these activities have been identified as commonly used and illustrate how to use the system.

3.10.1 Legal control

All the functions in Section 3.10.1 can be reached through the Compliance and License Management sections of the FIORI Menu (see Figure 3.64).

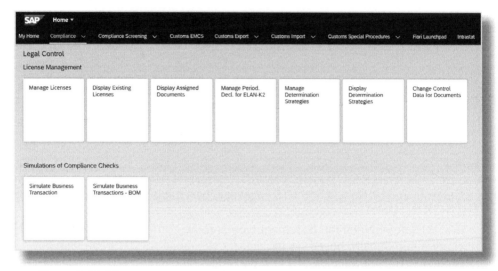

Figure 3.64: License management apps

Compliance Documents—Display Documents (Compliance Management)

When you enter this app, you are faced with a menu at the top. You can use this menu to narrow down your searches by many fields and functions. If you choose, you do not need to select or identify anything, and can leave the results wide open. If you do, you will see all documents with the block status and if the reason for block is due to:

▶ Missing data or other status issue

▶ Embargo

▶ SPL

▶ Export control

You can choose to view only those documents that are blocked for a specific reason or multiple reasons. You can also narrow your search by:

▶ FTO

▶ Legal regulation

160

- Year
- Date
- Document number

Regardless of the selection you make, you will be taken to a results screen (see the example in Figure 3.65).

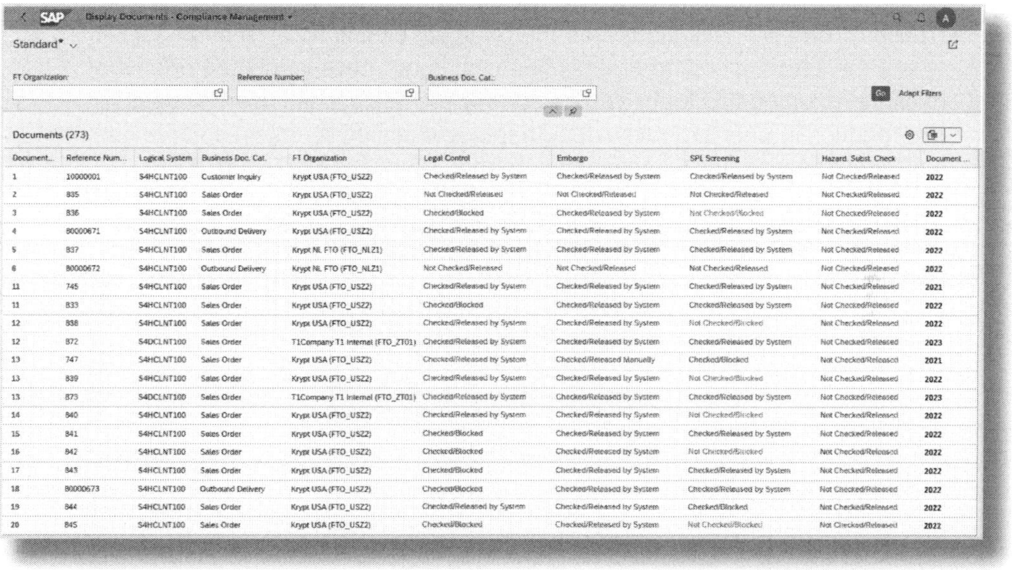

Document...	Reference Num...	Logical System	Business Doc. Cat.	FT Organization	Legal Control	Embargo	SPL Screening	Hazard. Subst. Check	Document ...
1	10000001	S4HCLNT100	Customer Inquiry	Krypt USA (FTO_USZ2)	Checked/Released by System	Checked/Released by System	Checked/Released by System	Not Checked/Released	2022
2	835	S4HCLNT100	Sales Order	Krypt USA (FTO_USZ2)	Not Checked/Released	Not Checked/Released	Not Checked/Released	Not Checked/Released	2022
3	836	S4HCLNT100	Sales Order	Krypt USA (FTO_USZ2)	Checked/Blocked	Checked/Released by System	Not Checked/Blocked	Not Checked/Released	2022
4	80000671	S4HCLNT100	Outbound Delivery	Krypt USA (FTO_USZ2)	Checked/Released by System	Checked/Released by System	Checked/Released by System	Not Checked/Released	2022
5	837	S4HCLNT100	Sales Order	Krypt NL FTO (FTO_NLZ1)	Checked/Released by System	Checked/Released by System	Checked/Released by System	Not Checked/Released	2022
6	80000672	S4HCLNT100	Outbound Delivery	Krypt NL FTO (FTO_NLZ1)	Not Checked/Released	Not Checked/Released	Not Checked/Released	Not Checked/Released	2022
11	745	S4HCLNT100	Sales Order	Krypt USA (FTO_USZ2)	Checked/Released by System	Checked/Released by System	Checked/Released by System	Not Checked/Released	2021
11	833	S4HCLNT100	Sales Order	Krypt USA (FTO_USZ2)	Checked/Blocked	Checked/Released by System	Checked/Released by System	Not Checked/Released	2022
12	838	S4HCLNT100	Sales Order	Krypt USA (FTO_USZ2)	Checked/Released by System	Checked/Released by System	Not Checked/Blocked	Not Checked/Released	2022
12	872	S4DCLNT100	Sales Order	T1Company T1 Internal (FTO_ZT01)	Checked/Released by System	Checked/Released by System	Checked/Released by System	Not Checked/Released	2023
13	747	S4HCLNT100	Sales Order	Krypt USA (FTO_USZ2)	Checked/Released by System	Checked/Released Manually	Checked/Blocked	Not Checked/Released	2021
13	839	S4HCLNT100	Sales Order	Krypt USA (FTO_USZ2)	Checked/Released by System	Checked/Released by System	Not Checked/Blocked	Not Checked/Released	2022
13	873	S4DCLNT100	Sales Order	T1Company T1 Internal (FTO_ZT01)	Checked/Released by System	Checked/Released by System	Checked/Released by System	Not Checked/Released	2023
14	840	S4HCLNT100	Sales Order	Krypt USA (FTO_USZ2)	Checked/Released by System	Checked/Released by System	Not Checked/Blocked	Not Checked/Released	2022
15	841	S4HCLNT100	Sales Order	Krypt USA (FTO_USZ2)	Checked/Blocked	Checked/Released by System	Checked/Released by System	Not Checked/Released	2022
16	842	S4HCLNT100	Sales Order	Krypt USA (FTO_USZ2)	Checked/Blocked	Checked/Released by System	Not Checked/Blocked	Not Checked/Released	2022
17	843	S4HCLNT100	Sales Order	Krypt USA (FTO_USZ2)	Checked/Blocked	Checked/Released by System	Checked/Released by System	Not Checked/Released	2022
18	80000673	S4HCLNT100	Outbound Delivery	Krypt USA (FTO_USZ2)	Checked/Blocked	Checked/Released by System	Checked/Released by System	Not Checked/Released	2022
19	844	S4HCLNT100	Sales Order	Krypt USA (FTO_USZ2)	Checked/Released by System	Checked/Released by System	Checked/Blocked	Not Checked/Released	2022
20	845	S4HCLNT100	Sales Order	Krypt USA (FTO_USZ2)	Checked/Blocked	Checked/Released by System	Not Checked/Blocked	Not Checked/Released	2022

Figure 3.65: Display Documents

This is a very useful screen to review documents and provides a snapshot of the blocks currently in the system. It is not, however, a comprehensive tool for releasing or dealing with these documents. If the block is for a reason such as SPL, restitution, or embargo, you will need to go back and go to another app to deal with the issue. Similarly, if the block is due to missing data, you will have to correct the data. If, on the other hand, the block is due to an export control license requirement, it can be dealt with right in this screen if certain conditions are met. Two possible scenarios are described below.

Scenario 1: Release the document by assigning it to a license.

If the document is blocked due to a license requirement, you can release the document in the RESOLVE DOCUMENT BLOCKS screen by assigning the document to a license. This assumes, of course, that the license is already set up. If no suitable license has been set up, you cannot resolve the issue in this area alone.

Provided the license exists, you can click on the RELATED APPS BUTTON (Related Apps) and click on the CHANGE LEGAL CONTROL DATA option.

This will take you to a screen that lists all of the available licenses and you can assign your document to one by clicking on the ADOPT LICENSE FOR ITEM BUTTON ( ). This illustrates the principle explained in Section 3.12.4 where the same user who creates licenses is not necessarily the one who uses them. Using this logic, you could only provide certain users access to this function in SAP GTS (view documents and assign licenses) and provide a different user exclusive access to creating licenses (see Figure 3.66).

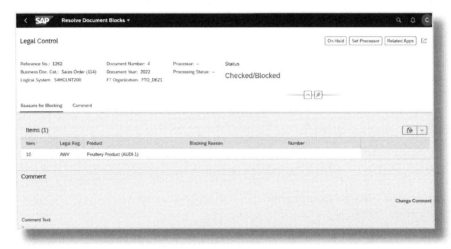

Figure 3.66: Blocked document release using direct license assignment.

Scenario 2: Release the document by changing the product classification

> **! Be very careful with classification changes**
>
> This scenario is one that should not be used unless the user is a compliance specialist who clearly understands the legal requirements. If the classification is wrong, then this may be an appropriate approach. However, if the user is wrongfully changing the classification just to release the document, you could end up in serious trouble.

The other way to release a blocked document in the review blocked documents screen is to change the classification of the product. Let's look at the scenario.

The user has entered the MANAGE BLOCKED DOCUMENTS screen (see Figure 3.67) and sees that a document is blocked for a license check. When they click on the DETAILS button (›), they see the reason for this block. In this case, the reason is that classification 7-3.6.m to Mexico requires a license under the Canadian Export Controls (EARCA) regulation (see Figure 3.68).

Figure 3.67: Manage Blocked Documents

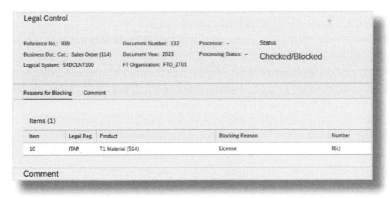

Figure 3.68: Details of legal controls block

At this point, the user could change the classification of the product if they know that 7-3.6.m is incorrect. As warned, this must not be done unless the user is certain that he or she is making the correct, compliant choice. To do so, go to the MANAGE PRODUCTS App and adjust the classification. Once this step is complete, click on the RECHECK DOCUMENTS App.

We cannot state enough that this function must be used with caution.
We recommend that you restrict access to this function to prevent errors.
In fact, we mention the function here more as a warning rather than as a
suggestion. Now that you are aware of this function, you can prevent its
misuse.

Export licenses—Create/maintain export licenses

The MANAGE LICENSES function has three options: create, change, display.

When you create a license, you will be taken to the menu shown in Figure
3.69 that allows you to choose the LEGAL REGULATION and LICENSE TYPE.
Furthermore, you can select an existing license to use as a template.

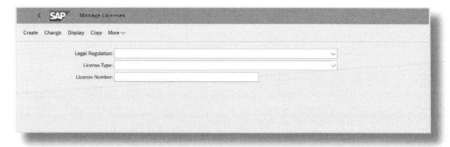

Figure 3.69: Create License

Once you have made your selections, you will be taken to the main license
screen (see Figure 3.70). There are several functions here; some of the key
ones are described below are the essential fields that will decide whether
your license is compliant or not. Please also see Section 3.12.1 for more
information on compliant license creation and use.

> **! Actual government issued license vs. internal controls**
>
> As has been discussed elsewhere, GTS license functionality can be
> used with government-issued licenses and permits, as well as with in-
> ternal controls not mandated by a regulatory body. The discussion be-
> low assumes that you have a government issued license. It is absolutely
> critical that you enter the contents of that license into GTS accurately!

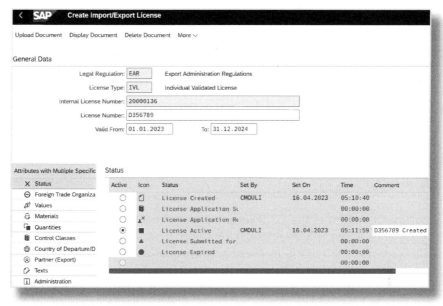

Figure 3.70: License Screen

LICENSE NUMBER: This must be the actual license number given to you by the government. It will appear on critical GTS-generated documents and communications, such as the export declaration.

VALID FROM: Ensure this value exactly matches the dates provided to you by the government. Most licenses cover a specific period of time, and GTS needs to know this.

QUANTITIES: This must be the exact quantity shown on your government license. For example, if they allow you to export 1000 liters of a particular chemical under the license, you must capture that here.

☛ Quantities in licenses

Check the unit of measure used in your product SKU and compare it to the unit of measure used in the government-issued license. For example, you may measure your product in SAP using "EA" (each), and the product is a five-gallon pail containing 18.9 liters. Your license allows 1000 liters of product to be exported. The quantity you will want to capture in GTS is 52 EA. This will be the most you can export without exceeding 1000 liters.

FOREIGN TRADE ORG. UNIT: This is critical: your license will belong to and be useful for a specific legal entity. Ensure sure that GTS knows which legal entity is allowed to use the license. Your company may represent multiple legal entities acting as a business group, but the license will be specific to one or more of them. Make sure you do not accidentally violate the terms of the license by improperly setting up FTO.

COUNTRY OF DEPT./DEST.: Enter the allowed country of departure or destination in this field. This will be the country you plan to trade with. For example, if your chosen FTO is in the US, this is the country you plan to sell to. You do not need to confirm the US because it is attached to the FTO. If the license is for exports to Mexico, you would enter MX.

CONTROL CLASS: Enter the ECCN or other classification number tied to the license in this field. For example, if your license is from the BIS to export 1C350.3.a-classified items to Mexico, you would enter that classification here.

This should wrap up your license creation stage. At some point, you will return to edit the license and assign a document or documents to it. Alternatively, the document assignation may happen in the DISPLAY BLOCKED DOCUMENTS screen as described above.

The actual license copy (pdf, jpg etc.) provided by government agencies can be attached to the license created in SAP GTS. You can use the upload document option to attach the document and display and delete to manage already attached documents (see Figure 3.71).

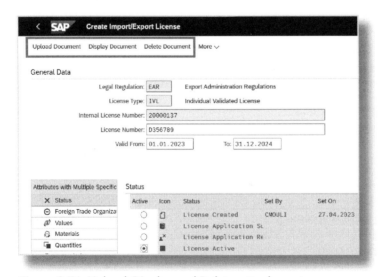

Figure 3.71: Upload, Display and Delete attachments

Embargo—release blocked documents

To release documents blocked for embargo, you would need to go to the MANAGE BLOCKED DOCUMENTS app (see Figure 3.67). The menu for MANAGE BLOCKED DOCUMENTS is quite large and allows you to filter/narrow it down by multiple factors such as:

- ▶ Legal regulation
- ▶ FTO
- ▶ Document number
- ▶ Date

If you are like most operations, you will be able to run this report without restrictions because embargo blocks are rare. However, depending on the unique needs of your organization, this may be a menu you need to spend more time on. Once you have made your choices, the results screen appears (see Figure 3.72).

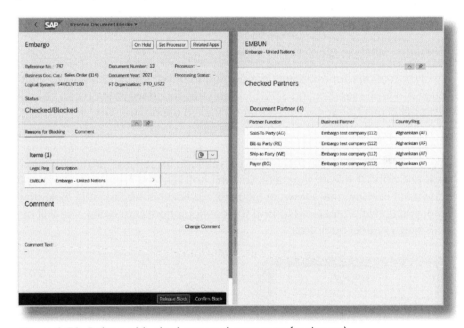

Figure 3.72: Release blocked export documents (embargo)

On this screen, you can review all the documents currently blocked due to an embargo. You can also release them.

> **! Be careful with embargo release**
>
> You must question why you would ever release an embargo block! If the embargo is legitimate, then you are likely forbidden from transacting with that country. Be very careful here.

To release the document, highlight it and click on the RELEASE BLOCK button (Release Block). You will be asked if you are sure and to double-check. Click on YES and you will go to the REASONS FOR RELEASE dialogue. Similar to the same function in SPL, you can choose a predefined reason and add notes or text to it.

As we will discuss in the compliance tips section (see Section 3.11), we recommend that you use licenses in situations where an embargo is not absolute. If you must release documents in the embargo screen, ensure that your compliance manager runs the ANALYZE REASONS FOR RELEASE report regularly as part of an audit program.

Embargo—analyze reasons for release

Analyze reasons for release is a reporting tool that should be part of your audit program (see Section 3.12.5). Using this functionality, you can see all user decisions to release an embargo-blocked document. You will also see the reason they chose at the time of release.

You will need to activate the catalog of reasons for release, or this function will not work. If this is the case, you will not see any options in the drop-down list like the one shown in Figure 3.73. For this reason, it is essential that you activate these reasons in the configuration. Otherwise, you will be missing a critical audit tool.

Figure 3.73: Reasons for release not active

3.10.2 Compliance management: Classification/master data

All the functions in Section 3.10.2 are accessed through the Products and Classifications sections in the Fiori menu (see Figure 3.74). There are many functions in this section, but we will focus on the classification of products. We will describe and compare the two key methods for classification (individually and worklist) and then describe a reporting/analysis tool.

> 👉 **Harmonized tariff numbers vs. export control numbers**
>
> The process for classification is very similar whether you are classifying an HS number or an ECCN number. This section will focus on ECCN because it is the compliance chapter. See the customs management chapter in the sequel to this book for more detail on HS number classification.

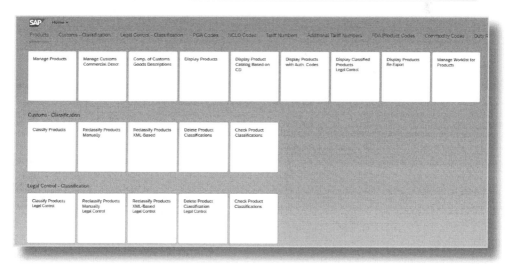

Figure 3.74: Products and Classifications

Classify via worklist

Under the CUSTOMS-CLASSIFICATION screen, you will find CLASSIFY PRODUCTS. This is a useful tool for classifying multiple products at once and can save time. However, it does not have the auditing tools that individual maintenance has.

When you click on this function, you will be taken to the CLASSIFY PRODUCTS menu (see Figure 3.75). The options in this menu define the worklist that you will see when you click on EXECUTE. Let's walk through some key options and fields on this screen.

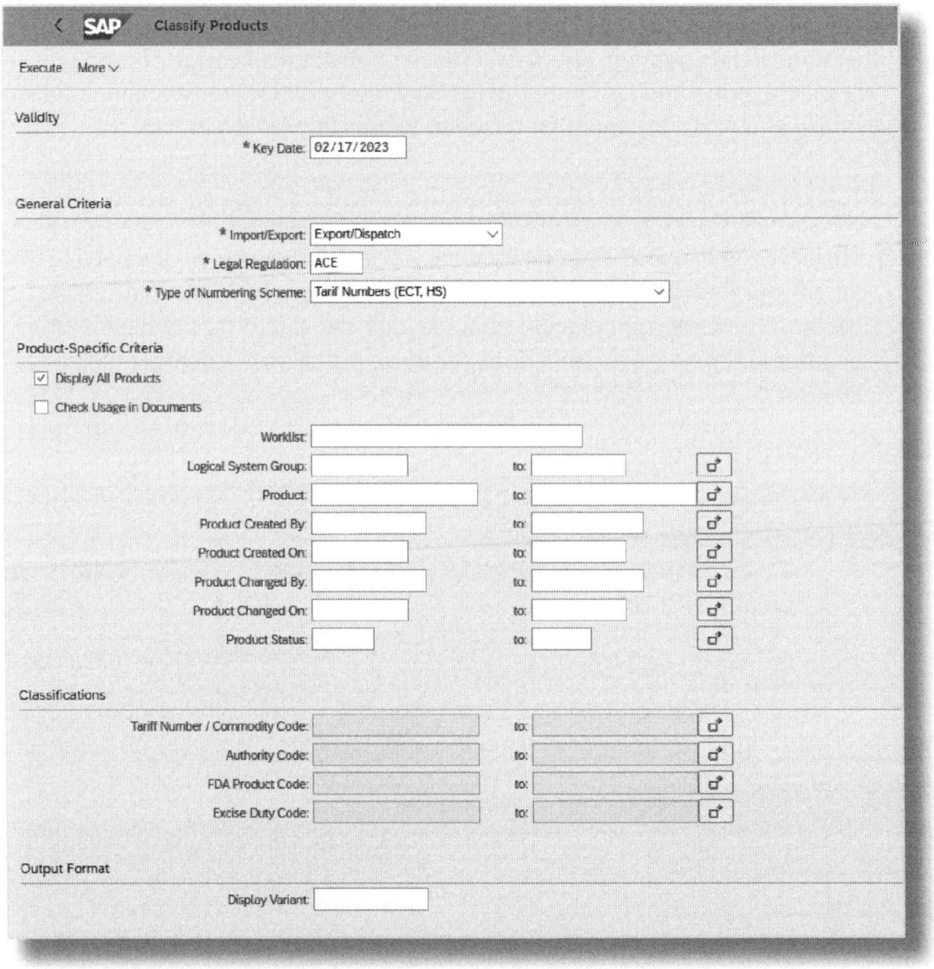

Figure 3.75: Classify products menu

IMPORT/EXPORT: Toggle between import control classifications and export control.

LEGAL REGULATION: Select an active legal regulation from the IMPORT/ EXPORT dropdown menu. The example in Figure 3.75 shows EXPORT/DISPATCH, ACE.

DISPLAY ALL PRODUCTS: Check this option to see products that are already classified, or leave it blank to see only products not yet classified.

PRODUCT: This can be a single product, a string of products, or a range. You can also enter a partial product code followed by an asterisk to see all codes that begin with that partial code.

PRODUCT CREATED ON: If your company is disciplined and maintains classifications of all new products, you can use this option to see recently created products only. For example, you can use this to see products classified within a recent timeframe, such as last week.

Once you have made your selections and click EXECUTE, you will be presented with a list of products filtered according to your selections. You can see an example worklist in Figure 3.76.

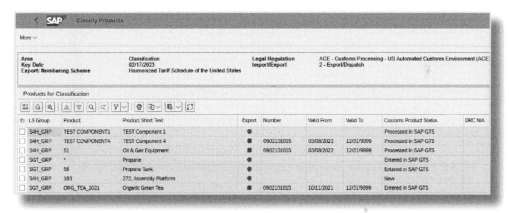

Figure 3.76: Worklist for classification

Once in the CLASSIFY PRODUCTS screen, you can classify products individually or as a group. The real power of this screen is to do so as a group. If you only need to classify one product, we recommend that you see the following section on individual maintenance.

To classify multiple products, highlight the ones you want to include and then click on the CLASSIFY PRODUCTS button (⊞).

You will be taken to a screen where you can assign the classification to those selected products (see Figure 3.77). Simply enter the desired classification and click the ⊞ button again. You will have classified as many products as selected in one action. You do not need to click save; it saves automatically.

171

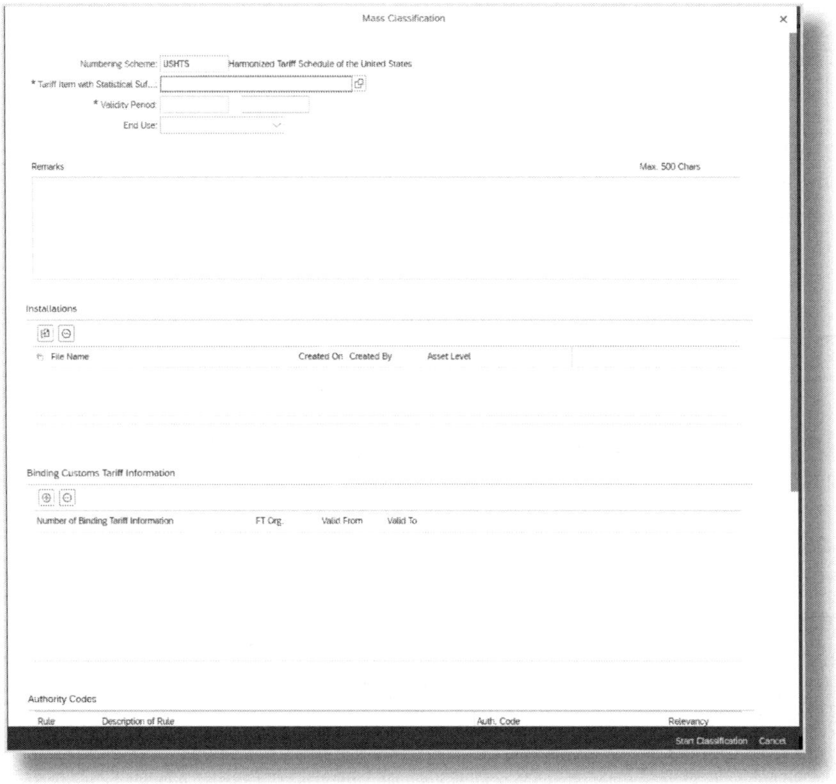

Figure 3.77: Assign multiple classifications

Manage products

Unlike the CLASSIFY PRODUCTS option, this method forces you to classify products one at a time. However, it gives you some more auditing and commentary tools, which is preferable when you are performing sensitive classifications.

The menu options are more robust than in the worklist option, but in practice, you probably know the product code you seek. If not, and you need to search for it with these fields and options, there are some good tools available (e.g., dates, grouping, short text). For this exercise, we will assume that you are entering a single product code, as shown in Figure 3.78.

When you click CHANGE, you will be directed to a screen like the one in Figure 3.79. You will want to go to the LEGAL CONTROL tab to edit a classification as shown in Figure 3.80, in addition to the key activities available on this screen.

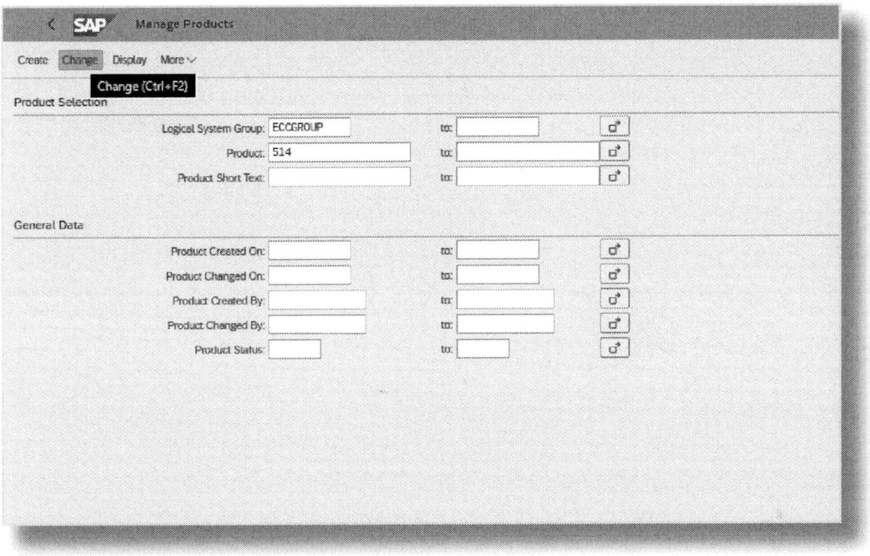

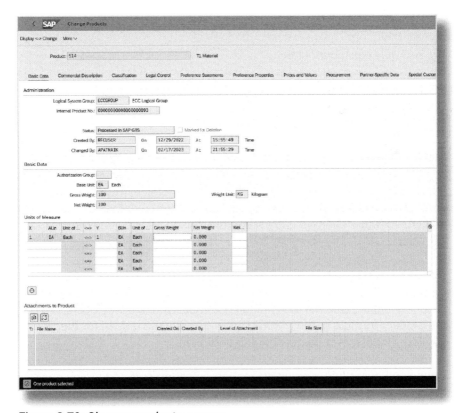

Figure 3.78: Manage products menu

Figure 3.79: Change products screen

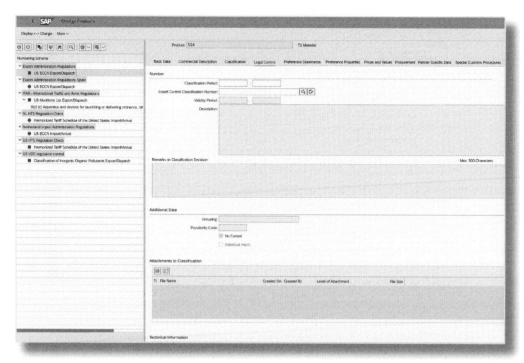

Figure 3.80: Legal control tab

ECCN: Choose and assign the classification for this product in this field. If you know it already, you can go ahead and enter it. If you are not sure, you can click on the FIND (🔍) button.

CREATE COMMENTS (✏). This is a useful tool where you can write a short comment. We advise making this a habit when performing sensitive classifications. For example, if you are classifying a chemical mixture containing Triethanolamine (TEA), you could state the exact percentage of TEA in the mixture so future auditors understand the reason behind your chosen classification.

ADD FILE (📎): This field is an even more powerful tool than the comments for audit trail purposes. You can upload a copy of any file or document you wish. Continuing with our TEA mixture example, you could upload a copy of the product formula or the MSDS. This will justify the reason for the classification should it ever be questioned or audited.

Once you have made your classification selection and added any desired documents or comments, click on SAVE, and you are finished.

Analyze product classification

This tool is found on the lower left side of the DISPLAY CLASSIFIED PRODUCTS (LEGAL CONTROL) menu.

This is a good tool for reviewing and auditing classification choices made by other users. It can also be useful for reviewing your own past classifications. The menu screen allows you to pull up results by various options and filters such as (see Figure 3.81):

▶ Product number/range of numbers

▶ Product description

▶ Product created/changed on date

▶ Product created/changed by user

▶ Legal regulation

▶ Classification number

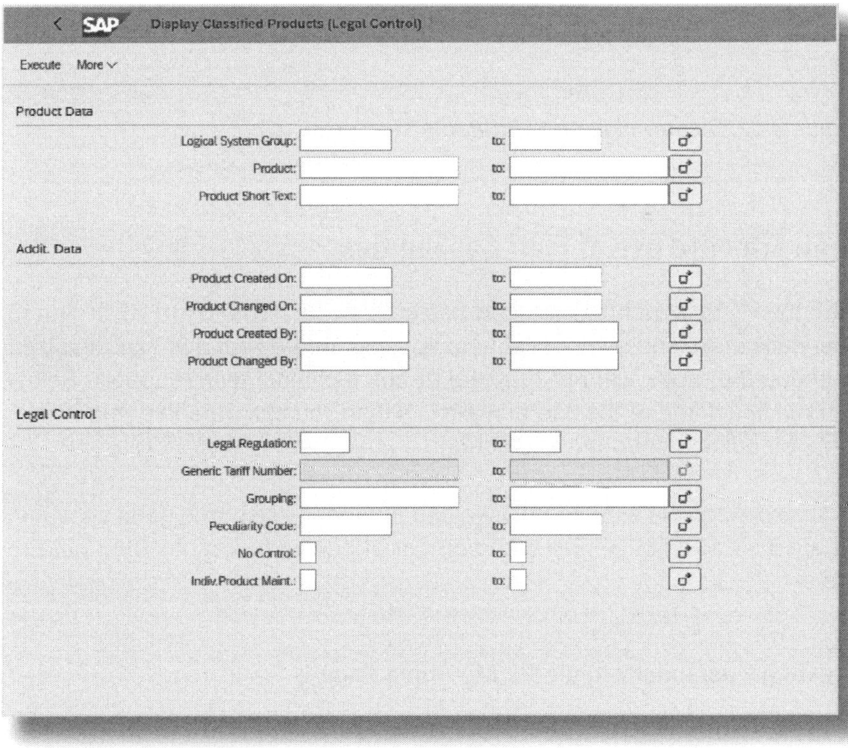

Figure 3.81: Display Classified Products menu

The results can be seen in Figure 3.82. In this example, we see several products and how they are classified over several legal regulations. As you can see, this is a powerful tool for reporting and auditing.

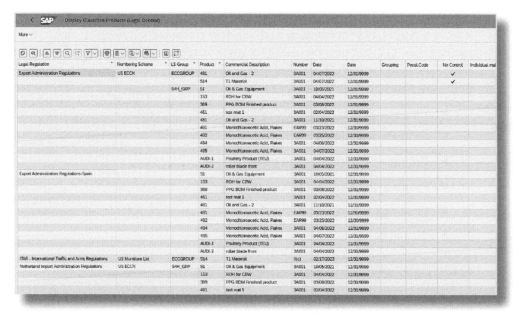

Figure 3.82: Display classified products

3.11 Effective use of Fiori Capabilities

With the FIORI launchpad you can customize your home page according to your daily tasks and responsibilities. You can create your own personalized dashboard of apps without the help of any technical team support. Below you will find some of the useful ways in which you can organize your homepage for quick monitoring and actions.

In this scenario we explore how we can personalize a home page shown in Figure 3.83 with active tiles with number of blocks by various filter parameters.

Creating a personalized tile for My Home Page

Access the manage blocked documents FIORI app. Choose the filter parameters as per your requirement. Once this is setup choose the icon SHARE ⤤ and choose option SAVE AS TILE and enter the details on the following

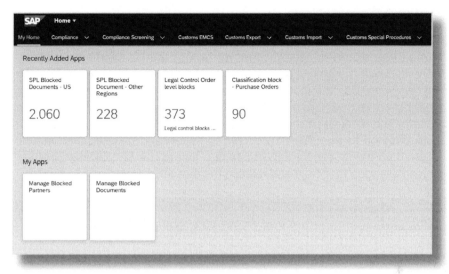

Figure 3.83: Personalized My Home Page

pop-up screen shown in Figure 3.84. Choose a title and select the pages as My Home. This tile will be available on my home page. The number of blocked documents automatically updates when you login and as you click the tile it will take you directly to the blocked document report with the selected filter parameters.

Figure 3.84: Save as Tile

Easy ways to share objects

If you have a blocked document or a partner which you need to review with a colleague or a compliance manager you do not need to send screen shots. Instead, out-of-the-box FIORI offers a way to share a link to the object you are reviewing. Use the icon ⬀ available on every FIORI screen and select SEND EMAIL. This will open a link to the email app which is configured in the system. The receiver of this email can simply click the link to be automatically directed to the SAP GTS screen to review and take required action. Figure 3.85 below shows how to share a link to the SPL blocked partner with a colleague to review and release the partner.

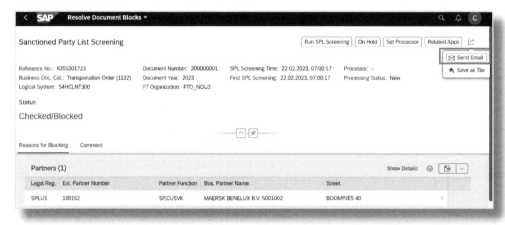

Figure 3.85: Send the blocked partner link as email to review

3.12 Compliance management tips

These are challenging times for companies that trade internationally. More than ever, regulations regarding import and export controls seem to be a moving target. Thankfully, SAP GTS is a flexible, responsive tool that can adapt to these changes instantly, provided the administrators are on top of the required changes.

In the following section, we will go through some tips and suggestions for using SAP GTS to ensure that you are always compliant.

3.12.1 Export compliance tips

Classification of products (subscription)

The first thing you must decide regarding classification is whether to use a subscription service. There are third-party companies that will offer you the complete list of possible classifications for particular export control programs. This will ensure that you always have the most current and complete list available.

This decision should be based on the number of varying classifications you plan to use. Let us use the US ECCN (Export Control Classification Number) as an example. There are hundreds of ECCN numbers that may apply to your products, and they are subject to periodic changes/reforms. This would be a difficult list to fully maintain without a subscription.

If you know that you have only three or four different ECCN that are relevant to your product mix, then you probably do not require a complete list. Manually setting up a few classification numbers is not a significant job. However, if you have a product mix that consists of dozens of classifications, or if your mix frequently changes, you may need a subscription to ensure you always have the current ECCN list.

This is really a business decision; you can operate with or without a subscription in a compliant fashion. You must weigh the time cost of maintaining the data vs. the hard cost of the subscription price.

One tip to consider: if you decide to maintain the classifications manually, ensure that your compliance staff work hand in hand with your IT team when the classifications are set up to ensure they are accurate. Similarly, your compliance staff will need to alert your IT team anytime the classification schedule changes, to ensure GTS is up to date.

Licenses and license exceptions

SAP GTS makes a license decision based on the classification of the product and the country of destination. For example, if a US company were to enter an order for a customer in Cameroon for a product classified as

1C350, it would require a license, whereas that same product would not require a license for Canada.

On a basic level, this is how licenses work: when a requirement for a license is found, the document is blocked until you secure the appropriate license and enter the data into SAP GTS.

Something to consider here is that most companies will limit the users who can set up a new license in GTS (See Section 3.12.4). Keep this in mind as you continue reading.

However, most regulatory bodies also have license exceptions. These are cases where a license is not required, despite the matching classification type and destination.

For example, US EAR allows a license exception for Tools of Trade (EAR 740.9(a)(1)) if they are going to be used by the shipper's employees in the destination country and either consumed or returned.

This raises two key questions:

1. How does GTS know if an exception applies?

2. How should this be handled in GTS?

The first question has a simple answer: GTS cannot possibly know this. A user will have to make the determination that the exception applies, which leads to the next answer.

The best way to handle this is to set up a license in advance for any exception you expect will apply to future shipments.

This will allow a user who has identified this exception to apply it to their document, without setting up a new license that could delay the shipment.

You can use a specific license type for these, such as EXCPT. This will make it clear to users and auditors that it is not an actual license but rather an exception.

We further recommend that you cite the license exception and make it clear that this is not an actual license. If you are audited later, internally or externally, it is important that this is clear and obvious so that the auditors can trust your system.

Figure 3.86 below shows a sample image of a license built to allow for the use of a license exception.

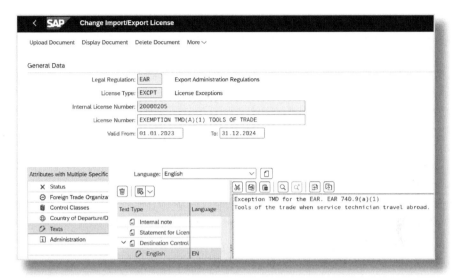

Figure 3.86: License exception example

Embargoes vs. license requirements

SAP GTS has embargo functionality that blocks all documents to or from a listed country. A common use for this is when US owned or based companies block all shipments to or from Cuba to comply with the Department of Treasury OFAC rules.

Most companies operate this way, and to ensure compliance, they simply forbid transactions with Cuba.

However, there are companies that do trade with Cuba and do so legally using licenses or license exceptions. The US embargo on Cuba is a constantly shifting landscape, and the last 10 years have seen both a loosening of restrictions, and then a return to a stricter embargo. Throughout all the changes however, there has always been some legitimate trade allowed with Cuba. How will GTS users manage this if Cuba is listed as an embargoed destination in their system?

SAP GTS does have a release function for embargos, as shown in Figure 3.87.

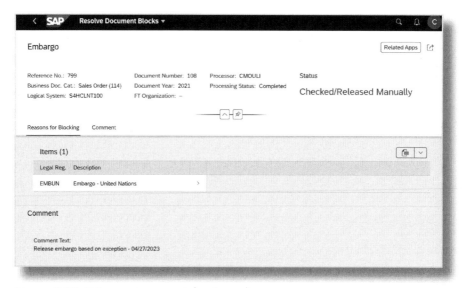

Figure 3.87: Release document (embargo)

However, this is not a very good system for audit purposes, as it only allows a simple text field explaining the purpose of the release. Furthermore, it does not factor in items or quantities and simply releases the document.

If you are a company that plans to take advantage of US licenses and exceptions for Cuba, then we recommend the following approach. Of course, this scenario can apply in any country related to any embargoed destination, but we are using US/Cuba to illustrate.

First, create a control in GTS that **all** product classifications require a license to Cuba. This is done in the maintain determination strategy function.

Typically, licenses are required for specific ECCN/country combinations. Many ECCN classifications can export to most countries without a license. For this scenario, a license requirement will need to apply, regardless of classification, when the country is Cuba. Either this can be done by assigning all available classifications to the license determination or by creating an ECCN grouping that contains all ECCN within it.

This will cause all documents to Cuba to be held for a license check and allow the user to determine if this is a valid use of a license and/or exception. This way, a proper audit trail will exist, and it will be a more transparent process than simply releasing the embargo on the document. This will also allow for quantity deprecation, which embargo functionality does not.

Reexport concerns

SAP GTS has robust re-export functionality. This allows you to maintain control after it leaves your original country, provided the business in the destination country is also on SAP GTS.

This kind of *extraterritorial control* is found in multiple US rules. For explanation purposes, we will use the EAR. More recently, China has become the second significant country to implement re-export controls. This could become a growing concern as time passes.

The US EAR rules extend control of products outside the territory of the USA. This can even be true if the US origin product is transformed or consumed into a new product in the second country. As a result, that second country may require a US re-export license when they ship that newly created product (that contained US content).

If the second country simply re-ships the US origin good in the same condition, it will absolutely be controlled, as if it was being exported from the USA.

Figure 3.88 is an image taken from the EAR regulations 15 CFR 736.2(b) (1). It explains that both exports and re-exports may require a license. This leads to the question, what is a re-export? The Bureau of Industry and Security (BIS), which governs the EAR, offers some explanatory material on its website (see Figure 3.89)[1]. Figure 3.90 and Figure 3.91 are from the same website and explain when a license may be needed for a re-export.

(1) *General Prohibition One—Export and reexport of controlled items to listed countries (Exports and Reexports).* You may not, without a license or License Exception, export any item subject to the EAR to another country or reexport any item of U.S.-origin if each of the following is true:

(i) The item is controlled for a reason indicated in the applicable Export Control Classification Number (ECCN), and

(ii) Export to the country of destination requires a license for the control reason as indicated on the Country Chart at part 738 of the EAR. (The scope of this prohibition is determined by the correct classification of your item and the ultimate destination as that combination is reflected on the Country Chart.)[1] Note that each License Exception described at part 740 of the EAR supersedes General Prohibition One if all terms and conditions of a given License Exception are met by the exporter or reexporter.

Figure 3.88: EAR 736.2(b)(1)

---

[1] "Guidance on the Commerce Department's Reexport Controls", accessed July 7, 2015, *https://www.bis.doc.gov/index.php/documents/licensing-forms/4-guidelines-to-reexport-publications*

What is a Reexport?

A *reexport* is the shipment or transmission of an item subject to the EAR from one foreign country (i.e., a country other than the United States) to another foreign country. A reexport also occurs when there is "release" of technology or software (source code) subject to the EAR in one foreign country to a national of another foreign country.

Figure 3.89: BIS—What is a re-export?

A. Determining whether a U.S.-origin item requires a license from BIS.

You may need to obtain a license to "reexport" an item that was produced or originated in the United States. Many items subject to the EAR do not need a license to be reexported from one foreign country to another. But certain items are controlled and will either require a license or must qualify for a License Exception. License requirements apply particularly to items controlled by multilateral export control regimes. In addition, some destinations and persons (individuals or groups) are subject to comprehensive export controls, including controls on widely traded consumer products.

Figure 3.90: US origin item may need license

B. Determining whether your foreign-produced product requires a license from BIS because it contains some U.S.-origin content.

As noted above, certain foreign-produced items are also subject to the EAR because they contain more than a specified percentage value of U.S.-origin controlled content. You need to first determine if your foreign produced item is subject to the EAR. If you determine your foreign produced item is subject to the EAR, you will then follow the process outlined in Part A above to determine if your foreign-produced item requires a license.

Figure 3.91: Foreign produced product may require a license

Let's walk through a simple process flow to illustrate how this may look. Figure 3.92 represents a US company exporting a product to its Canadian subsidiary. The Canadian subsidiary later re-exports that product to Russia. Remember, even if the Canadian company uses the US product to manufacture a completely new Canadian origin product, the re-export could still require a license. GTS allows you to construct these rules and will check the

Bill of Material in the Canadian system to look for controlled US product. For ease of illustration, in this example the product is re-exported without changes.

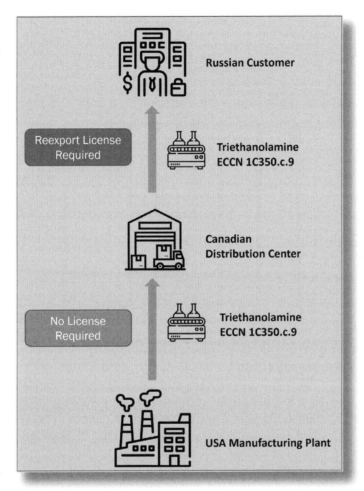

Figure 3.92: Re-export flow

You may notice that no license is required when the product ships from the USA to Canada, but a license is required when that same product ships from Canada to Russia. This raises a very serious area of risk for many North American companies.

Canada enjoys a privileged status with US regulatory bodies, such as the Department of Commerce. Very few products require a license when they ship from the US to Canada. Figure 3.93 shows what is called the Com-

185

merce Country Chart—Supplement No. 1 to Part 738 of EAR. If there is an "X" in the column, then a license is required when items of that category ship to that country. As you can see, very little requires a license to Canada, as opposed to other countries.

Commerce Control List Overview and the Country Chart														Supplement No. 1 to Part 738 page 1

Commerce Country Chart

Reason for Control

Countries	Chemical & Biological Weapons			Nuclear Nonproliferation		National Security		Missile Tech	Regional Stability		Firearms Convention	Crime Control			Anti-Terrorism	
	CB 1	CB 2	CB 3	NP 1	NP 2	NS 1	NS 2	MT 1	RS 1	RS 2	FC 1	CC 1	CC 2	CC 3	AT 1	AT 2
Afghanistan	X	X	X	X		X	X	X	X	X		X		X		
Albania[2,3]	X	X		X		X	X	X	X	X						
Algeria	X	X		X		X	X	X	X	X		X		X		
Andorra	X	X		X		X	X	X	X	X		X		X		
Angola	X	X		X		X	X	X	X	X		X		X		
Antigua & Barbuda	X	X		X		X	X	X	X	X	X	X		X		
Argentina	X					X		X	X		X	X		X		
Armenia	X	X	X	X		X	X	X	X	X		X	X			
Aruba	X	X		X		X	X	X	X	X		X		X		
Australia[3]	X					X		X	X							
Austria[3,4]	X					X		X	X			X		X		
Azerbaijan	X	X	X	X		X	X	X	X	X		X	X			

Export Administration Regulations	Bureau of Industry and Security	April 8, 2022

Figure 3.93: Commerce country chart

Because of this, there is a real danger for companies that operate primarily within the US and Canadian markets. They can fall into a pattern of never needing an export license because their trade is between the US and Canada, and no license is required. They may be caught unaware if, at some point, they open up business in new countries and begin exporting from Canada to those countries. They may not realize they are breaking US law because they were not educated or prepared for this eventuality.

Properly setting up GTS will protect your company and block shipments as necessary, whether this happens weekly for you or if it comes up once in ten years. When you do run into this situation, GTS will be ready, unlike a manual system.

3.12.2 Import compliance tips

Embargoes vs. license requirements

In Section 3.12.1 we discussed the use of embargo vs. license for a scenario when a US company exports to Cuba. The same situation can apply in an import scenario. While the previous discussion focused on exports, it is equally applicable to imports.

Using import licenses to manage quantity limits, substance lists, and quotas

Many countries have rules regarding how much of a given product can be imported. These rules can come from a variety of sources:

▶ Textile quotas

▶ Agricultural quotas

▶ Chemical inventories

▶ Other controlled products or chemicals (e. g., drug precursors controlled by the DEA in the US)

These rules are not truly a license requirement. If you import a quantity within the allowance, you are not required to report your activity. However, you must not import more than the permitted quantity. As an example, we will use the Canadian Domestic Substance List (DSL), which governs the import of chemicals that are new to the Canadian market. Very similar rules also exist in the EU with REACH.

If a chemical is on the DSL list, then it is considered part of the Canadian marketplace already. In other words, people are already making, importing, and/or using this chemical. If this is the case, there is no limit to how much you can import.

If, however, the product is not on the DSL list, then you face a more difficult scenario. Generally, you can import up to 1,000 kg of the product without any permit or notification requirement, but you must not import more than this amount without contacting Environment Canada.

There are then progressive stages of notification after that as you progress up to 10,000 kg and beyond.

How can you be sure you do not exceed these limits if you have identified a non-DSL product?

SAP GTS can help with this. You can set up an import license requirement for those products into Canada.

You can prearrange a standing 1,000 kg license, allowing GTS users to import up to that amount by assigning their documents to the license. Once they exceed that limit, their documents will be blocked until someone creates a new license in GTS. This will not be done until the required notification to Environment Canada has been made to allow import of up to 10,000 kg.

Since you will have separated user roles appropriately (see Section 3.12.4), this will allow the business to operate without interruption until you reach these limits, while also ensuring that logistics users cannot exceed them.

This is a way you can use SAP GTS import license functionality to ensure compliance of a non-license, quota-type regulation. As you review the countries you operate in, you will likely find many more scenarios like this where SAP GTS can help.

3.12.3 Classification compliance tips

Schedule B vs. HTS USA

The US maintains two separate versions of the Harmonized Tariff Schedule. One is called the *Harmonized Tariff Schedule of the United States (HTS US)* and is primarily intended for imports into the US. It has also been historically referred to as the Schedule A list. It is administered by the *US International Trade Administration Commission (USITC)*.

The other is called the *Schedule B*. It is administered by the US Census Bureau, Foreign Trade Division. This list is intended for reporting exports from the USA.

Many companies report their imports using the HTS US and their exports using the Schedule B.

When you implement GTS, assuming you intend to use both import and export functionality, you will need to decide whether to maintain both lists.

It is an ideal situation if you maintain only the HTS US list and use it for both exports and imports. This will save time and energy, as only one list must be updated and loaded.

This is perfectly legal according to 15 CFR 30.6(a)(12), which states that you can report either the Schedule B classification or the HTS US, with some exceptions (found in the "head note of the HTS US").

These exceptions are found in the Notice to Exporters section of the HTS US. Be sure to review this notice; it is a 12-page list of goods that cannot be reported for export using HTS US, but must use Schedule B. The list can be found here:

http://www.usitc.gov/publications/docs/tata/hts/bychapter/1500n2x.pdf

Provided you do not have any of these products, you should be able to use the HTS US for both imports and exports, saving a great deal of time and cost.

ECCN classification tips

The following discussion will focus on the US EAR ECCN system, but the same points can apply to any classification-based trade control system, such as:

▶ US Department of State ITAR Classifications

▶ Canadian Foreign Affairs Export Control List

▶ Australian Defense and Strategic Goods List

▶ Countless other country control lists

For explanation purposes, we will only look specifically at the ECCN system.

The US Department of Commerce is responsible for the Commerce and Foreign Trade Regulations, specifically 15 CFR 730 – 799. These are known as the Export Administration Regulations (EAR).

These regulations create a complicated product classification system. This is known as the Export Control Classification Number, or ECCN. The list they are maintained in is the Commerce Control List (CCL).

This classification is critical, as it drives the possible requirement for an export license, as well as various other regulatory mandates such as reporting.

SAP GTS, as has been discussed in this chapter, is a tool to ensure that you properly manage your ECCN-classified products. Once you set up the ECCN for a specific material master, you can use GTS to ensure you never fail to secure a license through document blocking.

However, GTS is a tool for managing products with an ECCN assigned; it cannot help with your ECCN classification process.

Here are some recommendations for your ECCN process, which will help ensure that you have a compliant system in place. Should you ever be audited by the US Department of Commerce, taking these steps will go a long way to ensure a positive result.

☛ ECCN Tip 1: Find expertise in your business sector

The CCL consists of many different products, ranging from obscure chemicals with names that are dozens of letters long to body armor, software, and infrared cameras! As a result, not very many people are "experts" in using the whole CCL. Someone who works in the chemical industry may be a specialist in those specific chemical controls, but will they know if your computer contains controlled encryption software? If you do not have the necessary expertise in-house, seek out third party assistance with specific CCL expertise related to your area of business. Do not pay a third party to classify your coated steel pipes if their specialty is rifle scopes.

☛ ECCN Tip 2: Make ECCN classification a required part of new product set up

The safest way to ensure proper classification of all your products is to require that all new product set-ups go through this step. If you allow new product set up to happen without it, on the assumption that "it will get done," you may find you have exported the good before you classified it and missed a critical license requirement. Do not allow new products in your system until they are classified.

☛ ECCN Tip 3: Do not only look at currently exported products

The CCL is relevant to more than just exports. You can also violate the EAR by allowing a foreign national to view the plans for creating your CCL controlled product simply as having them in your factory for a tour! Similarly, the US Department of Commerce identifies some people in the US that require a license for controlled products, and even though you did not export it, they are deemed a high enough risk that a license is needed. You will not know how sensitive your items are until you classify them. Furthermore, you may export tomorrow what you sell domestically today—do not get caught unaware; classify everything!

☛ ECCN Tip 4: Review past classifications regularly

Most manufacturing companies alter their formulas, plans, designs, etc. over time. In other words, the same product may be made slightly different today than it was last year. To give a chemical example, you may currently use Triethanolamine (TEA) in your chemical mixture, which triggers a 1C350 control, and you have set up the appropriate products in GTS with that classification. At some point, your R&D learns that an alternate to TEA is available, and they change the formula. Your product no longer requires the 1C350 classification; do you have internal systems that will catch this and make the required change? This can apply to other areas such as electronics. Imaging cameras are classified according to very precise specifications such as number of pixels and wavelengths. If you alter the specification, you could change the classification. For these reasons, it is essential that a product is not only reviewed once in its lifetime but is also subject to periodic reviews.

☛ ECCN Tip 5: Monitor changes To EAR and impact on your products

Similar to Tip 4, there is another reason for mandating reviews of existing classifications. The classifications themselves can change over time. The US Department of Commerce periodically alters, edits, removes, and adds classifications. You need to be aware of these changes and review the impact on your existing classification decisions. GTS can help with outright classification additions and deletions, assuming you have a subscription service that will be updated. If you had previously classified a product, and that classification number no longer exists, GTS has tools to assist with this called re-classification. Sometimes, however, the Department of Commerce will not change the classification but rather the criteria within it. For example, in 2014, several toxins previously classified under 1C360 were moved to 1C351. You need to be responsive to these types of changes, which can only happen through regular reviews.

☞ ECCN Tip 6: Take care not to assume EAR 99—Product nature vs. use

A common mistake made by companies during the classification stage is exclusively focusing on the content or material nature of their products. As a result, the company assumes their product is EAR99 (not controlled) simply because it is not specifically listed in the CCL. However, the use, purpose, or design of your product can also trigger a classification, and this is not always appreciated. The most commonly known use is the classification of goods "specially designed" for military use. However, less commonly understood purposes could place a good in a classification other than EAR99. For example, an otherwise EAR99 "harmless" item can become classified if it is "specially designed" for use with nuclear plants. Even paint could be classified, if it is designed specifically for use in a nuclear plant. This is the subject of an actual multimillion-dollar penalty you can view publicly! Other things to watch for are products and equipment designed to operate at extreme depths or for use with aviation.

☞ ECCN Tip 7: Document your classification process

Above all, document everything! All of your products should have a short file that describes the process that was used to determine classification. BIS considers robust compliance plans a mitigating factor should you be found in violation of a rule. In other words, having a robust plan and failing is better than never trying. It will have a material impact on penalties and enforcement. Documenting your formal classification process and the specific decision tree used on each product is an essential part of any compliance program.

3.12.4 User roles

SAP GTS Edition for HANA provides a range of predefined user roles that can be assigned to users based on their responsibilities and level of access needed. Each of these user roles is designed to provide access to specific functionality within SAP GTS Edition for HANA, allowing users to perform their assigned tasks efficiently and effectively while maintaining the security and integrity of the system. The following is a list of some of the key user roles available in SAP GTS Edition for HANA:

Classification Specialist: SAP_BR_CLSFCTN_SPCLST_LLS This user role is responsible for managing product classification, classification content, and special classification codes.

Compliance Analyst: SAP_BR_CMPLNC_SPCLST_LLS This user role is responsible for performing compliance-related tasks such as screening business partners, generating compliance reports, and managing compliance workflows.

EMCS Specialist: SAP_BR_EMCS_SPCLST_LLS This user role is responsible for managing and reporting excise goods movement under the Excise Movement and Control System.

Export Customs Specialist: SAP_BR_EXPORT_SPCLST_LLS This user role is responsible for managing customs-related activities such as export declaration, duty calculation, and customs clearance.

Import Customs Specialist: SAP_BR_IMPORT_SPCLST_LLS This user role is responsible for managing Import customs-related activities such as import declaration, duty calculation, and customs clearance.

Intrastat Specialist: SAP_BR_INTRASTAT_SPCLST_LLS This role involves managing Intrastat reporting requirements for all intra-European Union (EU) trade. Ensuring compliance with Intrastat regulations, Managing data and fixing discrepancies before filing it to customs.

Free Trade Agreement Specialist: SAP_BR_PREF_SPCLST_LLS This user role is responsible for maintaining and issuing customer and vendor certification, managing various free trade agreement qualification analysis.

Trade Compliance Specialist—Screening: SAP_BR_SCRNG_SPCLST_LLS This user role is responsible for maintaining and managing the SPL screening process. This includes screening and releasing blocked partners and documents.

Customs Specialist—Special Procedures: SAP_BR_SP_PROCED_SPCLST_ LLS This user role is responsible for managing customs-related duty savings programs activities such as import/export declaration for special procedures like Bonded Warehouse, Processing Under Customs Control, Foreign Trade Zones etc.

The new pre-delivered roles work very well and they offer a good base framework if your organization has complex security needs. We can make some suggestions and observations based on experience on how you can build the new roles.

We have grouped the roles by user activities:

- ▶ Configuration
- ▶ Periodic User Roles
- ▶ Master Data Maintenance
- ▶ Daily User Roles

The very first thing to consider when developing your strategy is the size and complexity of your organization. If, for example, you have 50 different products and average one license requirement a year, you can probably assign nearly all the roles to one person! If, on the other hand, you have thousands of products and require a license every week, the roles will need to be split up out of necessity as well as for compliance purposes.

Some suggestions related to each role group are provided below.

Configuration

Most companies follow the generally accepted best practice that configuration is kept separate from the user experience. IT or "SAP Specialists" generally have sole access to SAP GTS configuration, and the users who manage functional activities cannot go into configuration.

This is because the activities in configuration are critical and sensitive; misuse or an incorrect action can cause the entire system to fail.

Everything deemed "configuration" for the purpose of this discussion is found outside the SAP GTS FIORI launchpad, in the "SPRO—Customizing" section. All discussions after this refer to functions found in the FIORI launchpad of GTS.

Periodic user roles

This category covers functions found in GTS that are performed infrequently and are very critical and/or sensitive. Improper use of these sections will cause GTS to be ineffective for your compliance needs.

Setting up and maintaining classification numbers can be done manually or through a subscription service. Either way, it is essential; it is one of the key drivers of license determination.

The other key driver in license determination is the determination strategy. This is where you tell the system which countries require a license for which classification type.

Due to the infrequency and sensitivity of this function, we recommend that this function fall to someone other than the daily users. This individual should be from the compliance part of your business, perhaps a compliance manager or someone in with a similar role. This way, all the changes made will be made by someone who understands the importance and meaning of their work.

Master data maintenance

There are as many ways to handle master data maintenance as there are types of master data! Bottom line? You need to trust that the data is accurate and complete. How you get there is up to you.

Here we are specifically referring to classification of products (e. g., setting them up with an ECCN number). An ideal best practice is one where the actual individual or individuals who make your classification determination are the same ones who set them up in GTS. This way, there is no chance of miscommunication. The individual setting up the classification in GTS is the one who decided what it should be.

This may not be realistic, of course. You may have a compliance manager determining classification who does not have time to set up each product.

In this case, the compliance manager may need to hand the duty to a trusted subordinate or another GTS user. The classifications could be fed to the subordinate via email or a file. This approach is not as, but it is the reality for many companies.

Daily user roles

Lastly, we get to the heart of the compliance workload in GTS—reviewing blocked documents, setting up licenses, and assigning documents to licenses.

Having users perform all of these roles can work perfectly adequately, but we suggest one separation. Creating licenses and assigning documents should belong to a more limited number of users than the review of blocked documents.

Reviewing a blocked document is a fairly low-risk task by itself. The user will notice that a license is required and alert the necessary managers or experts. These experts should have exclusive rights to create a license and assign the document to it because this is sensitive work.

Alternatively, if your company has many license requirements, you could restrict access to license creation but allow many users to assign documents to those licenses.

As previously stated, there are many ways to develop a user role strategy. Just be sure you give yours adequate thought and planning and that it is a compliant, efficient model for you.

3.12.5 Auditing your compliance program

You will want to implement routine audits of your compliance system. There are multiple components and aspects to the system as discussed above, and due diligence requires you to audit its effectiveness. By "system," we do not simply mean "SAP GTS." We mean the comprehensive, global system around GTS, from configuration through subscription services to end user training. Below we provide a high-level overview of the compliance chain. A weak link or break anywhere in this system could cause failure and non-compliance. Each one of these sections must be audited periodically.

Suggested areas to audit

Classification of products

▶ Are all products classified when a new product is set up?

▶ Who decides classification?

▶ Is the classification process documented?

Ongoing review of classifications

▶ Are all classified products reviewed periodically to see if the classification is still valid for that product?

▶ Are changes to the classification system implemented and the impact on your products reviewed?

Activation of SAP GTS functionality

▶ Were all necessary aspects of compliance activated and defined?

Communication with the ERP system

▶ Are all necessary documents transferring to GTS for a compliance check?

▶ Are compliance blocks in GTS resulting in blocks in the ERP system?

▶ Are ERP users alerted to blocks when they occur?

▶ Verify that change pointer program to transfer new or changed master data (customer, vendor and material master) is working?

Configuration settings

▶ Are the configuration settings right for your needs?

▶ Are the settings periodically reviewed and adjusted as needed?

▶ Do you periodically simulate a license requiring transaction and verify a positive result?

User Decisions

▶ Are licenses (past and present) audited for compliance to ensure user-performed licenses are set up appropriately?

> ▶ Do you test the license program, attempting to exceed quantity limits and recording result?

> ▶ Are user roles assigned according to strategy developed by compliance management?

System Health Check

> ▶ Are system logs for data loads reviewed periodically?

> ▶ Are the audit logs captured for compliance area periodically archived?

> ▶ Are all the organization parameters, such as new plants or storage locations, created in ERP system in sync with GTS?

4 Appendix 1: SPL list types and references

The table below provides common lists that businesses screen against. The list codes are from Descartes (MK Denial) and are used with permission. Next to each list code is a description explaining what the list is, in addition to a website users can go to for further information.

This is meant to be a tool that you can incorporate into your company's SPL compliance program. When you have a potential match against one of these lists, you can go to the website to gain a better understanding of:

▶ If you have a true match, and

▶ What the significance of the list is.

This table is not a complete list of SPL offerings. It is intended to show the most common and most important lists, and to assist you as you customize your own internal training program. Since lists change frequently (some are delisted and new ones are created) this is not meant to be a static tool—you must review it and keep it updated constantly. It is our hope that this will give you the start of a good tool and point you in the right direction.

List	Description	Direct website link to source list and information
231RU	CAATSA Section 231(e) (DOS)	*https://www.state.gov/caatsa-section-231d-defense-and-intelligence-sectors-of-the-government-of-the-russian-federation/*
561L	List of Foreign Financial Institutions (OFAC)	*http://sdnsearch.ofac.treas.gov/*
ACL	Australian Consolidated List	*https://www.dfat.gov.au/international-relations/security/sanctions/consolidated-list*
ATFMW	ATF & Explosives Most Wanted	*https://www.atf.gov/content/ATF-most-wanted*
AULTO	Australian Listed Terrorist Organizations	*https://www.ag.gov.au/national-security/australias-counter-terrorism-laws/terrorist-organisations*
BALK	SDN, Western Balkans (OFAC)	*http://sdnsearch.ofac.treas.gov/*

List	Description	Direct website link to source list and information
BOE	Bank of England—Financial Sanctions (HM Treasury)	https://www.gov.uk/government/publications/financial-sanctions-consolidated-list-of-targets
CBW	Chemical Biological Weapons Concerns (DOS)	https://www.state.gov/key-topics-bureau-of-international-security-and-nonproliferation/nonproliferation-sanctions/
COTED	Specially Designated National Cote d'Ivoire(OFAC)	http://sdnsearch.ofac.treas.gov/
CTL	Canadian Restricted Entities	https://www.international.gc.ca/world-monde/international_relations-relations_internationales/sanctions/current-actuelles.aspx?lang=eng
DEAMW	Drug Enforcement Administration	https://www.dea.gov/fugitives
DOS	Department of State Debarred Parties	https://www.pmddtc.state.gov/ddtc_public?id=ddtc_kb_article_page&sys_id=c22d1833dbb8d300d0a370131f9619f0
DTO	Designated Terrorist Organization (DOS/OFAC)	http://sdnsearch.ofac.treas.gov/
ERL	End-User Requiring License-Entity List (BIS)	https://www.bis.doc.gov/index.php/component/docman/?task=doc_download&gid=2911
EUS	European Union Sanctions List	https://www.eeas.europa.eu/eeas/european-union-sanctions_en
FBI	FBI Most Wanted List	http://www.fbi.gov/wanted
FINC	Money Laundering Concerns (FINCEN)	https://www.fincen.gov/
GSA	GSA Debarred bidders list	https://sam.gov/search/
INPA	Iran Non-proliferation Act (DOS)	http://www.state.gov/t/isn/c15231.htm
INPOL	Interpol—Wanted Persons	https://www.interpol.int/How-we-work/Notices/View-Red-Notices
ISA	Iran Sanctions Act (DOS)	http://www.state.gov/t/isn/c15231.htm

List	Description	Direct website link to source list and information
ISNA	Iran and Syria Non-proliferation Act	*http://www.state.gov/t/isn/c15231.htm*
MT	Missile Technology Concerns (DOS)	*http://www.state.gov/t/isn/c15231.htm*
MVC	Merchant Vessel, Cuba (OFAC)	*http://sdnsearch.ofac.treas.gov/*
NPWMD	Non-proliferation Weapons Of Mass Destruction	*http://sdnsearch.ofac.treas.gov/*
NSPLC	Non-SDN Palestinian Legislative Council (OFAC)	*http://sdnsearch.ofac.treas.gov/*
RFC	Red Flag Concerns (BIS Unverified List)	*https://www.bis.doc.gov/index.php/ policy-guidance/lists-of-parties-of- concern/unverified-list*
SDGT	Specially Designated Global Terrorist SDGT (OFAC)	*http://sdnsearch.ofac.treas.gov/*
SDME	Specially Designated Terrorists—SDME	*http://sdnsearch.ofac.treas.gov/*
SDNB	Specially Designated Nationals, Belarus (OFAC)	*http://sdnsearch.ofac.treas.gov/*
SDNC	Specially Designated Nationals, Cuba (OFAC)	*http://sdnsearch.ofac.treas.gov/*
SDNK	Specially Designated Nationals, N. Korea (OFAC)	*http://sdnsearch.ofac.treas.gov/*
SDNL	Specially Designated Nationals, Libya (OFAC)	*http://sdnsearch.ofac.treas.gov/*
SDNLB	Specially Designated Nationals, Lebanon (OFAC)	*http://sdnsearch.ofac.treas.gov/*
SDNLR	Specially Designated Nationals, Liberia (OFAC)	*http://sdnsearch.ofac.treas.gov/*
SDNR	Specially Designated Nationals, Iran (OFAC)	*http://sdnsearch.ofac.treas.gov/*
SDNS	Specially Designated Nationals, Sudan (OFAC)	*http://sdnsearch.ofac.treas.gov/*

List	Description	Direct website link to source list and information
SDNSO	Specially Designated Nationals, Somalia (OFAC)	http://sdnsearch.ofac.treas.gov/
SDNSY	Specially Designated Nationals, Syria (OFAC)	http://sdnsearch.ofac.treas.gov/
SDNT	Specially Designated Narcotics Trafficker	http://sdnsearch.ofac.treas.gov/
SECO	Swiss Restricted List	https://www.seco.admin.ch/seco/en/home/Aussenwirtschaftspolitik_Wirtschaftliche_Zusammenarbeit/Wirtschaftsbeziehungen/exportkontrollen-und-sanktionen/sanktionen-embargos/sanktionsmassnahmen/suche_sanktionsadressaten.html
TCO	Transnational Criminal Organisations (OFAC)	http://sdnsearch.ofac.treas.gov/
TDO	Denied Persons List (BIS)	https://www.bis.doc.gov/index.php/policy-guidance/lists-of-parties-of-concern/denied-persons-list
UKPC	UK Proliferation Concerns (Concern List Only)	https://www.gov.uk/international-non-proliferation-and-arms-control-regimes
UNS	United Nations Security Council Sanctions	https://www.un.org/securitycouncil/content/un-sc-consolidated-list
WB	World Bank — List of Disbarred/Ineligible Firms	http://www.worldbank.org/debarr

5 Appendix 2: Website resources

The following lists of websites are publicly available sites, where you can research various relevant topics. They are sorted by key categories. This list will be useful as you perform your master data set up and classifications. It will also lead you to sites that further explain various concepts discussed in this book.

5.1 Sanctioned party list resources

Hyperlink	Description	Country
https://www.trade.gov/consolidated-screening-list	Three Agency Consolidated Screening List (Downloadable)	USA
https://sdnsearch.ofac.treas.gov/	Department of Treasury Search Tool	USA
https://www.sam.gov	GSA Debarred Entity Search Tool	USA
https://www.un.org/securitycouncil/content/un-sc-consolidated-list	Security Council Sanctions (Downloadable)	UN
https://www.eeas.europa.eu/eeas/european-union-sanctions_en	EU Sanctioned Parties (Downloadable)	EU

5.2 Preferential trade resources

Hyperlink	Description	Country
https://can-mex-usa-sec.org/secretariat/index.aspx?lang=eng	USMCA Secretariat	North America
https://www.acquisition.gov/	Federal Acquisition Regulation (FAR)	USA
http://www.dot.gov/highlights/buyamerica	Buy America Requirements	USA

Hyperlink	Description	Country
https://www.ftc.gov/tips-advice/business-center/guidance/complying-made-usa-standard	FTC "Made In USA" Require-ments	USA
https://www.cbp.gov/document/guidance/side-side-comparison-free-trade-agreements-and-selected-preferential-trade	US List of Free Trade Agreements (Side by Side)	USA
http://ptadb.wto.org/	WTO Preferential Trade Page	UN
https://policy.trade.ec.europa.eu/eu-trade-relationships-country-and-region/negotiations-and-agreements_en	EU Free Trade Agreement Page	EU
https://www.international.gc.ca/trade-commerce/trade-agreements-accords-commerciaux/agr-acc/index.aspx?lang=eng	Canada List of Free Trade Agree-ments	CA

5.3 Export/import control resources

Hyperlink	Description	Country
http://www.bis.doc.gov/index.php/licensing/commerce-control-list-classification/export-control-classification-number-eccn	BIS ECCN Clas-sification Page	USA
https://www.bis.doc.gov/index.php/regulations/export-administration-regulations-ear	Export Administra-tion Regulations	USA
https://deccs.pmddtc.state.gov/deccs?id=ddtc_public_portal_itar_landing	Department Of State ITAR Page	USA
https://laws-lois.justice.gc.ca/eng/regulations/sor-89-202/FullText.html	Canadian Export Control System	CA
https://policy.trade.ec.europa.eu/help-exporters-and-importers/exporting-dual-use-items_en	EU Export Con-trols Page	EU
http://www.wassenaar.org/	Wassenaar Ar-rangement Page	Multi.
http://www.australiagroup.net/en/index.html	Australia Group Page	Multi.

5.4 Customs compliance resources

Hyperlink	Description	Country
http://www.cbp.gov/	US Customs And Border Protection	US
http://www.cbsa-asfc.gc.ca/	Canada Border Services Agency	CA
http://ec.europa.eu/taxation_customs/index_en.htm	EU Customs Union	EU
http://www.wcoomd.org/	World Customs Organization	UN

A About the Authors

Rajen Iyer, CTO ArchLynk is an entrepreneur and investor in innovative solutions and products with a passion for developing solutions that solve real-life supply chain and global trade challenges. A thought leader with several in-depth articles, patents, and best-seller books and white papers on Supply Chain Solutions and Global Trade to his name, Rajen has attended many industry conferences as a speaker and panelist. As an avid learner, curious in knowing and discovering new ways for applying emerging technologies in the enterprise world, Rajen is enthusiastic about the immense opportunities within the supply chain space, addressing common and complex challenges that have a real-world business impact to pave the way to success.

Kevin Riddell, CCLP, CCEP is the Director, Trade & Regulatory Compliance for the Tremco CPG Group, where he has worked for more than 25 years. The Tremco CPG Group manufactures and exports chemical-based construction products worldwide. Kevin is responsible for International Trade Compliance, including Customs Compliance and related import and export regulations. Kevin is the global business lead and administrator for SAP GTS and led the software selection/implementation process in 2011.

Kevin lives in Toronto, Canada. He is a regular presenter on SAP GTS as well as Trade Compliance, and he speaks at both SAP and non-SAP events. He is a volunteer with ASUG, America's SAP User Group.

Mouli Venkataraman is an accomplished Managing Director of Global Trade Practices at ArchLynk, with over 18 years of expertise in SAP GTS consulting and more than 22 years of experience in business software design, development, and deployment. He has an impressive track record of working on several large businesses and digital transformation projects, where he has excelled in designing and deploying complex trade compliance processes across diverse industry sectors. Mouli is highly regarded for his exceptional leadership skills, also leading ArchLynk's product and innovation team with remarkable success. Prior to his current role, Mouli served as a lead developer in the core GTS development team at SAP Labs, where he contributed significantly to the development of GTS 3.0 to GTS 10.1 versions.

B Index

C Disclaimer

This publication contains references to the products of SAP SE.

SAP, R/3, SAP NetWeaver, Duet, PartnerEdge, ByDesign, SAP Business-Objects Explorer, StreamWork, and other SAP products and services mentioned herein as well as their respective logos are trademarks or registered trademarks of SAP SE in Germany and other countries.

Business Objects and the Business Objects logo, BusinessObjects, Crystal Reports, Crystal Decisions, Web Intelligence, Xcelsius, and other Business Objects products and services mentioned herein as well as their respective logos are trademarks or registered trademarks of Business Objects Software Ltd. Business Objects is an SAP company.

Sybase and Adaptive Server, iAnywhere, Sybase 365, SQL Anywhere, and other Sybase products and services mentioned herein as well as their respective logos are trademarks or registered trademarks of Sybase, Inc. Sybase is an SAP company.

SAP SE is neither the author nor the publisher of this publication and is not responsible for its content. SAP Group shall not be liable for errors or omissions with respect to the materials. The only warranties for SAP Group products and services are those that are set forth in the express warranty statements accompanying such products and services, if any. Nothing herein should be construed as constituting an additional warranty.

More Espresso Tutorials Books

Rajen Iyer, Hariharan Subramanian

Transportation Charge Management in SAP S/4HANA®

▶ Transportation Charge Management processes

▶ Charge Management master data

▶ Strategic freight procurement and sales

▶ Settings and configuration

http://5530.espresso-tutorials.com

Kevin Riddell, Rajen Iyver:

Practical Guide to SAP® GTS, Part 2: Preference and Customs Management

▶ Best practices for leveraging SAP GTS for trade compliance

▶ Fundamentals of preference implementation and system set up

▶ How self-filing, broker models and free trade agreements can improve ROI

▶ Review of Version 11.0 with screenshots

http://5134.espresso-tutorials.com

Ashish Galchaniya, Rajen Iyver:

Practical Guide to SAP® GTS, Part 3: Bonded Warehouse, Foreign Trade Zone, and Duty Drawback

▶ Leveraging and configuring bonded warehouse

▶ Fundamentals of foreign trade zones

▶ How business users can get the most out of GTS functionality

▶ Detailed configuration and user guides for bonded warehouse and foreign trade zones

http://5162.espresso-tutorials.com

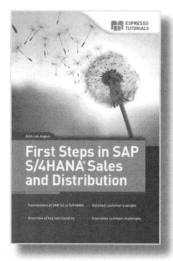

John von Aspen:

First Steps in SAP S/4HANA® Sales and Distribution (SD)

▶ Foundations of SAP SD in S/4HANA

▶ Sales orders and document types

▶ Master data objects, business partners and material masters

▶ Examples and screenshots based on a case-study approach

http://5353.espresso-tutorials.com